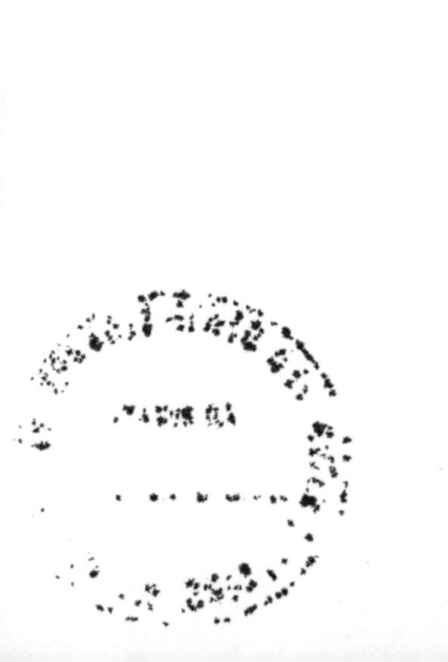

THE CATHOLIC PRIESTHOOD TODAY

by DONALD W. WUERL

FRANCISCAN HERALD PRESS
1434 West 51st St. • Chicago, Ill. 60609

LEO DEHON LIBRARY
P.O. BOX 429
HALES CORNERS, WI 53130-0429
25407
W952

THE CATHOLIC PRIESTHOOD TODAY by Donald W. Wuerl, copyright ©1976 by Franciscan Herald Press, 1434 West Fifty-First Street, Chicago, Illinois 60609. All rights reserved.

Library of Congress Cataloging in Publication Data:

Wuerl, Donald W.
The catholic priesthood today.
Bibliography: p.
1. Catholic Church—Clergy. 2. Priesthood—History of doctrines. I. Title.
BX1912.W83 253'.2 75-31791
ISBN 0-8199-0591-7

Nihil Obstat
GUNDISALVUS GRECH O.P.
Angelicum University, Rome

Imprimatur
HUMBERTO CARDINAL MEDEIROS
Archbishop of Boston

March 25, 1976

MADE IN THE UNITED STATES OF AMERICA

Preface

The title of Father Wuerl's book — *The Catholic Priesthood Today* — might at first jar those who are used to thinking of the concept of the Catholic priesthood as perennial, the very core and unchanging principle of the heart of the life and cult of the Catholic community. Why the qualifying word "Today"?

The author's own introduction promptly faces up to this difficulty and throughout the book he often makes it clear why one can and, indeed, must discuss the contemporary problems and current concept of the timeless priesthood of Christ though in terms, to be sure, of a permanent commitment by Christ Himself to those ordained in His own ministerial role.

Moreover, the priestly ministry is explored and explained by the author precisely in terms of the deliberations of the specific recent Synod, a Synod of "today" dedicated in great part to discussion on and study of the nature of the ministerial priesthood as it acts and reacts in the circumstances of our own day while remaining, in all its essentials, an unchanging reality, with a unique permanence and transcendence, a "reality" of union with Christ expressed in what is called a "character." To this permanent priestly "character," present only in the ministerial priesthood, so the author argues on the basis of the Vatican Council documents, as well as of Scriptural doctrine not always explicitly developed in the Synod, the priest is configured to Christ both ontologically and functionally and renders present to the end of time the permanent salvific presence among mankind of the Sole High Priest of the new law, Christ Jesus.

The presence in the title of the book of the word "Today" does not indicate, by the Mercy of God and the prudent preference of the author, that the present book is in any sense another sociological treatise on "The Priesthood in a Changing World." Of such there has been a surfeit; fortunately this abundant body of literature is now being supplemented, in great part because of the Synod, by serious theological discussion of a priesthood that is ultimately a theological reality rather than merely the object of sociological and psychological influences for better or worse. Father Wuerl's book is a refreshing addition to that ancient discussion for the same reasons that the Synod theme, which the author chose to synthesize and review, was so timely and profitable.

It is an effort, as was the Synod itself, to put the

ministerial priesthood back in its central place in the consciousness that the Church has of itself and its members.

It might well be concluded from what has just been said that the book is of interest only to priests. This, of course, is not true. Please God, it will be of interest to innumerable potential candidates to the ministerial priesthood who have lost heart or interest as a result of the "theological fatigue," to use the author's phrase, that has plagued so many articles, books, sermons, and discussion on the priesthood. The author, recalling the mass of inadequate or distorted theological output on the origins and the nature of the ministerial priesthood, accurately observes that it has cruelly afflicted believers within the Church. "Where theological exactness or even basic doctrine is pushed aside for a flourish, an ill-begotten headline, or a quick piece of notoriety, the whole Church suffers," he notes. This was largely the condition for a full generation prior to the Synod and this is what in some instances has happened even since as a result of an ill-considered appeal to an imagined "spirit" of the Council rather than to the actual documents of Vatican Council II.

One who takes the trouble to link the teaching of the Synod to the actual teaching of the Council will early discover the proper place of the concept of the priesthood in the mind of the total Church. He will not be tempted to isolate the ministerial priesthood, unique though it be, from the rest of the Body of Christ. He will not forget that there is a priesthood of the laity, nor will he fail to appreciate its dignity and modern-day urgency. There are even those of us who entertain the conviction that the beleaguered Church of the last part of the twentieth century will quite probably be "saved" by the laity, but at every turn in the ordinary operations of the Church and its Holy Spirit, the laymen depends on the functions and essential role of the ordained priest. This is true not in any "clericalist" sense, but by the very nature of things in the sacramental Church that Christ has in fact instituted as the normal means of the preservation and promotion of sanctity and to the salvation of souls.

Neither, of course, will the intelligent reader be inclined to isolate inaccurately the organized institutional Church, with its ministerial priesthood, from the general operation of the Holy Spirit in the salvation of those whom St. Augustine described as seeming far from us visibly, but really one with us invisibly. The presentation of the Catholic concept on this point did not need to wait for the Synod nor even the Council; it was luminously developed by Pope Pius XII in his letter on the so-called "Boston heresy," and in the last century Pope Pius IX wrote a letter which has its place in the bibliography of reflection on the salvation of those outside the Church.

Finally, even if Father Wuerl had developed more fully the implications of the Synod discussions concerning the question of celibacy in the contemporary priesthood, no one could possibly argue that he has denigrated the Holy Sacrament of Matrimony by his proper emphasis on the particular sanctity and special participation of the Ministerial Priesthood in the work of Christ. One mentions this only because there has been so much tendentious rhetoric concerning the Catholic understanding of the respective possibilities of sanctity and the presence of Christ in two sacraments, Holy Orders and Holy Marriage, which have historically become for many reasons and in most places distinct to the point of the practical exclusion of one another. The same St. Paul who described marriage as a great mystery in Christ and the Church is the St. Paul to whom we are indebted for the clear notion of the unique manner in which the Eucharistic Sacrifice is identified with the ministerial priesthood and constitutes its proper and permanent place in the redemption of mankind and the renewal of the world. Confusion on these points has never been without factionalism or the effort to establish a point which, like the roses that bloom in the springtime, has nothing to do with the case.

Father Wuerl lends a topical touch to his book on the concept of the priesthood today by linking part, at least, of his doctrine based on the Synod to the contentions of two authors whose books have enjoyed wide readership in recent times. One is the somewhat sensational book in which Professor Hans Küng appears to raise the question of why there should be priests at all. The other is the more recondite book of Father Raymond Brown, confined to Biblical reflections of a strictly exegetical character, which would admit that the concept of the priesthood today is probably valid enough, but is a post-New Testament development.

With regard to Father Brown, Father Wuerl contents himself with pointing out that the Sulpician author is confining himself to his own highly delicate professional field of exegesis and only by implication touching that wider field of faith and theology from which, however, even exegesis or any other branch of Sacred Science can never be entirely disassociated. His consequent conclusions concerning Father Brown's work are therefore less trenchant than the conclusions of Cardinal Shehan, of which Father Wuerl is, however, careful to take note. His criticism of Dr. Küng are necessarily more severe and sweeping, but he will seem to most readers kinder to the elusive German-Swiss theologian than is Küng's own compatriot and friend, Father Karl Rahner.

The inclusion of discussion of these two books adds an element of theological excitement, not without timely instruction, to the book itself. But its value does not lie in this excitement; it lies in the presentation from an authoritative source of the essential elements of the concept of that Catholic Priesthood so widely misunderstood and disastrously neglected today, even in the Church. No more important subject could have been chosen for the exercise of the talents of the author and of his own vocation as a priest.

John Cardinal Wright

VATICAN CITY,
April, 1976

Contents

Introduction

THE PURPOSE IN writing this book is to study the Church's present-day teaching about the Catholic priesthood, as seen in the Second Vatican Council and — more recently — expressed by the Third Synod of Bishops.[1]

This is a subject which calls for some clarification, not only for purely theological reasons, but also because objective study may help to dissipate the atmosphere of crisis which sometimes surrounds any discussion of the priesthood.

It will hardly be denied that the crisis now facing the Catholic priesthood is a real and serious one. It seems to me to have two aspects, the first being simply statistical. During the last few years, there has been a universal and steady decline in the number of young men offering themselves for the priesthood; at the same time, there has been a parallel increase in the number of priests seeking official laicization or — in some cases — abandoning their priesthood without bothering to go through that procedure. These tendencies have received much publicity and are well known. Nonetheless, a few figures may help to make the picture clear.[2] In 1967, the number of young men applying to enter major seminaries in Germany was 603; in 1969, the number was 461. The corresponding figures for France are 810 and 567. Over the same period, the number of major seminarians in the Netherlands (secular and religious, including novices) fell from 1,725 to 986; these figures reflect the sharpest decline in Europe, but they are rivaled by those for the United States, where 45,379 seminarians dwindled during those two years to 33,900.

The same tendency is reflected in the number of ordinations. If we consider the three years from 1966 to 1969, we find ordinations declining from 144 to 77 in Canada, from 91 to 45 in Austria, and from 566 to 345 in France. And behind all such figures there lies a story of seminaries emptying and being closed down — most rapidly of all in the Netherlands, with France close behind. The ranks of the priesthood are simply not being replenished on the old scale.

They are also being depleted by many departures. The official process of laicization is handled by the Congregation for the Doctrine of the Faith, and in 1971, that Congregation published some disconcerting figures.[3] In 1964, it received 640 requests for laicization; in 1966 it received 1,418; in 1969 it received 2,963. To such figures of canonically-authorized departures there must always be added the further numbers of those who have "just left." It has been estimated that in the United States and Canada, the net total of all such departures in 1968 amounted to 1.32% of all the clergy.

The overall picture is a clear one, and it invites speculation as to the causes of so uniform a trend. For one type of journalist, writing for one sort of public, the answer is obvious: celibacy is at last being recognized as an impossibility for the individual and an absurd stipulation on the part of the Church. There may be some truth in this; but I, for my part, find it hard to believe that celibacy is a *prime* factor except in a very few cases. If it deters some young man from the seminary, if it causes some older man to leave the priesthood, this will nearly always indicate some deeper difficulty about the Faith in general or the priesthood in particular. The same is true, I suspect, of a second explanation which is frequently offered in this generation, described once in a document by the United States Bishops as "aphrodisiac."[4] The publication of *Humanae Vitae* in 1968 is said to have made the pastoral task impossible; it is even said to have made traditional Catholicism untenable. Either way, the priesthood loses its attraction. This seems to me a more plausible explanation than that based upon the requirement of celibacy. But it is a very partial explanation at the most. Like that other, it presupposes some weakness in faith and, in particular, some reluctance to face the fact that Christian discipleship and good living necessarily involve a penitential and even crucifying element. *Humanae Vitae* merely reminded the Church of that painful but familiar truth, under one specialized aspect; in itself, it can hardly be seen as a major factor in the statistical crisis of the priesthood.

Vocation and priesthood are not merely patterns of human behavior; they are also operations of divine grace, and as such, they lie beyond our understanding. We shall never really *know* why the graph turns up in one century and down in another.

This brings me to the second and non-statistical element in the crisis. About priesthood, as about much else in theology, there has been a great deal of writing and talking since the Council, and in order to get things in proportion it is necessary to remember that much of this is sound and scholarly and in full continuity with Catholic teaching, adding up to an entirely legitimate process of "development" in Newman's sense of the word. But some of it has a very different character. Certain theological writers and speakers have recently been advancing views of the priesthood which are not in continuity with Catholic teaching — views which also show a marked tendency to be ill-thought-out and unscholarly. And the trouble is that it's these bizarre ideas which get the publicity. It's "news," it's a "story" when Father X or Doctor Y advances his own extravagant notion of the priesthood, but it's a boring and un-newsworthy fact that the great majority do nothing of the sort. Hence, from a thousand magazine articles and television interviews and news items and so forth, people get the impression that the active and real and important thinkers are these distinctly extravagant ones. And thus the impression is created that the traditional Catholic belief about the priesthood is in the melting pot.

This, of course, does not apply only to the priesthood. Many other aspects of the Church's actual thinking and explicit teaching get misrepresented in the same way. But its consequences here are particularly unfortunate. These "new" theologians differ widely in the detail of what they say. But the overall drift of their message is remarkably uniform: broadly, it is to the effect that the

Catholic priesthood isn't what we used to think it was. It has moved from a sacramental ministry to a social ministry. Its roots are not in divinely instituted Orders but in the momentary functional needs of a given congregation of believers.

It would be easy — but perhaps not very profitable — to illustrate this fact by a great many quotations. Here we will look at only a few typical ones. Fr. John W. Glaser, S.J., wrote an article in *Commonweal* under the title "Anonymous Priesthood."[5] In this article he tells us of a conversation which he had with a sister who had some difficulty in finding a priest to say Mass for the convent at a convenient time. The answer was obvious: he recommended that she say Mass herself. He goes on to tell us that

> "there are numerous priests in Catholic communities who are not called priests — who would not call themselves priests — nor would they be called priests by the laity nor by ecclesiastical authority. They are nonetheless, according to this theory, priests. I do not mean this merely in terms of the priesthood of the faithful; I mean that degree of explicit priesthood by which a man or woman has a right and duty to stand in a position of leadership in the faith community — liturgically, sacramentally and otherwise."

For Fr. Glaser, there is no objective difference between the priesthood of the faithful and the ministerial priesthood. Anyone who feels called to Christian leadership is — by that fact alone — made into a "priest" in the fullest possible sense of the word: he or she needs no ordination, no conferring of a specific sacramental character and power; there is no distinctive sacrament of Orders. The Second Vatican Council was wildly mistaken about this matter — as was the entire Catholic Church, during the two millenia of its existence.

Such thinking is not a private eccentricity of Fr. Glaser — or perhaps I should say, of Person Glaser. It is a minority view, beyond all doubt, but it is the view of a very vocal minority. Let me quote another of its members. Fr. Michael Richards wrote an article in the English *Clergy Review* under the title "Ministry, Sacrifice, Celibacy, and the Future."[6] "There are baptized Christians, confirmed Christians, ordained Christians," he tells us very truly; but

"all bear a character, the character of Christ, and none of these is any more priest, prophet or king than anyone else, because all are equally members in Christ of the New Israel. There is no difference of degree in their priesthood, any more than in their status as prophets or rulers."

He continues:

"The 'essential difference' conferred by ordination is not a difference of degree within the general priesthood of all; it is a difference of representation, of function and of service."

Richards continues:

"It is as much a mistake to regard him above all as a *sacerdos* as it would be to think of him exclusively as a prophet or a king; it is a mistake to think of him as a *sacerdos* in any sense in which the other members of the People of God are not equally *sacerdos.*"

Despite the questionable grammar, the message is clear, and it is much the same as that of Fr. Glaser. This line of thinking finds its fullest brief statement, perhaps, in *Why Priests?* by Dr. Hans Küng.

I have mentioned just one or two instances of a tendency which is fairly widespread but which comes to seem very widespread because of the selective publicity already mentioned. Countless people have thus acquired a vague but powerful impression that the Church has lost faith in its own priesthood, as once understood. In so far as such ideas get around, it is hardly surprising that vocations should dwindle. The image of the priesthood is not a clear one. And no one wants to give his life, energies and talents to a way of life that seems to be without purpose.

The need of the hour, as stated by the 1971 Synod, is to put into clear focus the Church's understanding of the priesthood. Here, by studying the documents on the priesthood which teach what the Church believes, I hope to help in some small way to dissipate a little of the intellectual confusion and the theological smog that has gathered around this subject.

Attempting to do so, I shall rely on two sources, the documents of Vatican Council II and *The Ministerial Priesthood* of the Third Synod of Bishops. In the course of the Church's long history of theological development, the status of a General Council and the reliability of its teaching have become well-defined and clear. The same is not true, however, of that recently-restored institution, the international Synod of Bishops. The exact theological weight of its statements is still a matter much discussed. And I shall touch on that later in this book. This question is yet to be worked out fully. I take it as obvious, however, that the Synod has at least *some* degree of teaching authority, does in *some* sense speak with the mind of the Church; and for my present purpose, I therefore think it important to pay very close attention to what the Third Synod actually said about the priesthood, as well as to what the Council had said previously. Thereafter, for illustration rather than in any spirit of mere contention, I propose to compare the teaching of the Council and the Synod with the views put forward by two writers, Fr. Raymond Brown and Dr. Hans Küng.[7]

One might almost ask whether a further statement on the priesthood was really needed. Objectively speaking, I am not sure that it was; that is, while the doctrine of priesthood is subject to development, its principal elements have not been in doubt for a very long time. But the appearance of doubt has certainly been created in recent years. In practice, therefore, the need for a reaffirmation by the Church of the teaching on the nature and function of the priesthood was most needed.

The Church has spoken, with at least a high degree of authority and with great clarity. In the following pages, I intend to analyze what it said about the priesthood, the ordained ministry of love and service.

NOTES

1. Dogmatic Constitution on the Church, Pastoral Constitution on the Church in the Modern World, Decree on the Bishops' Pastoral Office in the Church, Decree on Priestly Formation, and the Decree on the Ministry and Life of Priests. These documents along with all the other documents of Vatican Council II are found in English in the translation found in *The Documents of Vatican II,* editor Walter M. Abbott, S.J., (America Press, New York, 1966), and *Ministerial Priesthood,* Second General Assembly of the Synod of Bishops (1971) which synod is also the third in the series of synods since the document *Apostolica Sollicitudo.* The other synods were held in 1967, 1969 and the most recent, 1974.

2. Sources for all these statistics are the *Tabularum Statisticarum Collectio,* Secretariate of State, Central Office for Church Statistics, 1971, and the *Prospective,* Brussels, PVM, 1972.

3. *Ibid.,* Tabularum.

4. *Church in Our Day,* Collective Pastoral Letter, United States Catholic Conference, November, 1967, p. 49.

5. "Anonymous Priesthood," John Glaser, *Commonweal,* December 11, 1970, p. 271–74.

6. "Ministry, Sacrifice, Celibacy and the Future," Michael Richards, *Clergy Review,* January 1974, pp. 1–13.

7. Hans Küng, *Wozu Priester?* (Einsiedeln: Benziger, 1971), Translated by John Cumming (London: Collins, 1972).

1. The Council and the Priesthood

Of all the Councils held so far in history, the Second Vatican Council concentrated most heavily upon the nature and meaning of the Church. For some, it therefore deserved to be called "The Council on the Church." To say the least, two of its most frequently quoted documents — the *Dogmatic Constitution on the Church* and the *Pastoral Constitution on the Church* — are about the nature and function of today's Church, which is seen as the all-embracing context of all Christian life and witness. Any study of the priesthood must begin with this fact, and so I have chosen the *Dogmatic Constitution on the Church* to form the starting point for my brief study of the Council's teaching on the priesthood.

The first chapter of that Constitution speaks of the Church as a kind of sacrament, as an instrument by which God reaches man.

"By her relationship with Christ, the Church is a kind of sacrament or sign of intimate union with God and of the unity of all mankind. She is also an instrument for the achievement of such union and unity."[1]

This instrument or visible means is God's way of leading men to share in his divine life. There is no instrument distinct from this Church which so fully performs that function.

"This Church, constituted and organized in the world as a society, subsists in the Catholic Church, which is governed by the successor of Peter and by the bishops in union with that successor, although many elements of sanctification and of truth can be found outside of her visible structure. These elements, however, as gifts properly belonging to the Church of Christ, possess an inner dynamism toward Catholic unity."[2]

Furthermore, each of the individual sacraments is an expression in one way or another of the one great sacramental mystery which is the operation of the Church.

"It is through the sacraments and the exercise of the virtues that the sacred nature and organic structure of the priestly community is [sic] brought into operation."[3]

The Church, therefore, is the context of the priesthood, because it is the primary witness of Christ and has received the commission to preach the good news.[4] The

Church proclaims to all peoples the kingdom of Christ and witnesses his Resurrection before them, while also renewing his sacrificial and salvific death. As that same document puts it, Christ is the one Mediator, and his Church is his mystical body, created to continue his salvific work.

"Christ, the one Mediator, established and ceaselessly sustains here on earth his holy Church, the community of faith, hope, and charity, as a visible structure . . . For this reason, by an excellent analogy, this reality is compared to the mystery of the incarnate Word. Just as the assumed nature inseparably united to the divine Word serves Him as a living instrument of salvation, so, in a similar way, does the communal structure of the Church serve Christ's Spirit, who vivifies it by way of building up the body (*cf.* Eph 4:15)."[5]

According to the Council, the priest is consecrated — that is, set apart and differentiated from the rest of the community — by virtue of the Sacrament of Orders; and he is made into the image of Christ, the one and eternal High Priest.[6]

By sharing in the mystery of Christ, the priest shares in Christ's unique office of mediator; and for this reason he announces the word of God to all, and is particularly charged to introduce men into the People of God — that is, the Church — through baptism.

The Council continues that the priest exercises his ministry in the Eucharistic mystery where he acts in the person of Christ, proclaims the mystery of Christ, and becomes a true priest of the New Testament.[7]

Then, because of his priestly consecration, the priest is capable of reconciling sinners with God and with the Church through the sacrament of penance, and also by the sacramental anointing of the sick.[8] In this unique manner, the priest carries on the special work that was Christ's, using powers that Christ reserved to himself.

But this sharing in Christ's powers was not limited to the sacramental ministry, as the Council goes on to say. The priest also shares in the authority which Christ held as Pastor or Head of his Church. In his unique capacity as participator in the life and mystery of Christ, he is therefore charged to bring together the family of God,[9] and also to form and teach and lead this community on the path to salvation.[10]

The distinctive service of the priest lies in the exercise of his priestly duties. He is able to serve the community because he carries on the activities that Christ charged him to carry on. His service therefore begins with the preaching of the Gospel and reaches its culmination in the sacramental sacrifice of the altar.[11]

The Council concludes this first chapter by saying that the priest serves the glory of God and enriches the lives of men by his self-dedication in prayer and adoration, his preaching, his offering of the Eucharist, and his administration of the other sacraments.[12]

Another aspect is seen by pointing out that all the members of the Church are called to the one mission that was Christ's.[13] But the call makes different demands on different people, and some are called to participate in the specifically priestly work of Christ.

"Though they differ from one another in essence and not only in degree, the common priesthood of the faithful and the ministerial or hierarchical priesthood are nonetheless interrelated. Each of them in its own special way is a participation in the one priesthood of Christ. The ministerial priest, by the sacred power he enjoys, molds and rules the priestly people. Acting in the person of Christ, he brings about the Eucharistic Sacrifice, and offers it to God in the name of all the people."[14]

Individuals are therefore called out of the community by Christ, and later by his Church, the hierarchical structure of which is thus established. The Council points out in this chapter that it is the sacrament of Orders which differentiates members of the community and sets them apart for specifically ministerial priestly works. By baptism, one is set apart from the world and made a Christian; by Orders, one is set apart from the Christian community and made a priest.[15]

The Council goes on to speak of the various structures within the Church and explains in some detail the work of bishops, of priests and of deacons.

> "Although priests do not possess the highest degree of priesthood, and although they are dependent on the bishops in the exercise of their power, they are nevertheless united with the bishops in sacerdotal dignity. By the power of the sacrament of orders, and in the image of Christ the eternal High Priest (Heb 5:1–10; 7:24; 9:11–28), they are consecrated to preach the gospel, shepherd the faithful, and celebrate divine worship as true priests of the New Testament. Partakers of the function of Christ the sole Mediator (1 Tm 2:5) on their level of ministry, they announce the divine word to all."[16]

The priest, therefore, has a specific relationship to the Church — to the *entire* Church — specifically because of his vocation and ordination. He has been called to serve the People of God in a particular manner, he has been charged and empowered to edify them and so build up the entire mystical body of Christ. In this activity, he enacts and makes visible the living faith of the Church.[17]

If one wished, one could develop the theology found in the *Dogmatic Constitution on the Church* at great length, and show how it affirms that Christ's Church is his creation; that it exists to carry on his mission; that in order to do so effectively, it differentiates within its community; and that the principle of differentiation is that of Sacred Orders.[18]

The *Pastoral Constitution on the Church in the Modern World* applies the theology of the other and more dogmatic documents to the world of today. Its predominant theme — so far as the work, ministry, witness and role of the priest are concerned[19] — is the spiritual mission of the ministerial priesthood. The Council here faces some of the broader problems of today's world, and it is particularly clear about the spiritual character of priestly activity in the section which deals with political participation by the Church and her ministers today.[20] Here the Council is repeating once again what the Church has long held: that the role of the priest is that of spiritual leader in his community.

I shall not develop this theme here, but I shall refer to its practical application in a later chapter about Christian leadership, the priest as community builder, and the priest's involvement in partisan politics.

There are three other Council documents which shed a great deal of light on the Church's understanding of the priesthood. I cannot pass over these without mentioning them, even though — as I have said — this is only a brief survey of points that are very evident in the Council document. The *Decree on the Bishops' Office in the Church,* the *Decree on the Ministry and Life of Priests,* and the *Decree on the Church's Missionary Activity* all reinforce the essential theme that the Church is the witness of Christ, as he was the witness of the Eternal Father. They also point out that through the ministerial priesthood, this witness is shared in a specific and particular manner. For anyone interested in looking more closely at the mission and office of the bishop and his relationship with his priests, the *Decree on the Bishops' Pastoral Office* offers much material. Here particularly we see the Church's insistence on the unity of Holy Orders and the root of that unity in Christ's priesthood which all in Orders share.

> "All priests, both diocesan and religious, participate in and exercise with the bishop the one priesthood of Christ and are thereby meant to be prudent cooperators of the episcopal order . . . they form one presbytery and one family, whose father is the bishop . . . The relationships between the bishop and his diocesan priests should rest above all upon the bonds of supernatural charity so that the harmony of the will of the priests with that of their bishop will render their pastoral activity more fruitful."[21]

I will develop this point in a later chapter in the context of the Synod.

The Church in a particular way is the object of the priest's ministration because of the special relationship that each priest has — through his bishop — to the Church. The document on the pastoral office of bishops points out that the priest can sanctify the Church because he participates in the unique priesthood of Christ, and that in his activities he is exercising the same priesthood.[22] This point is repeated and confirmed in the *Dogmatic Constitution on the Church,* where the Council again points out that the priest acts in the very person of Christ in the Eucharistic sacrifice; so also in the document on the life and ministry of priests. Here we read that the priest is called to participate in Christ's priesthood; that he can sanctify the Church because he truly participates in the one priesthood of Christ; and that he acts as the minister of Christ in the celebration of the sacred mysteries.

The *Decree on the Ministry and Life of Priests* heavily emphasizes the witness mission of the priest. This theme also was handled by the Synod and will be considered in a later chapter of this book.

"Priests gather God's family together as a brotherhood of living unity, and lead it through Christ and in the Spirit of God the Father. For the exercise of this ministry, as for other priestly duties, spiritual power is conferred upon them for the upbuilding of the Church.

"In achieving this goal, priests must treat all with outstanding humanity, in imitation of the Lord. They should act toward men, not as seeking to win their favor, but in accord with the demands of Christian doctrine and life. They should teach and admonish men as dearly beloved sons, according to the words of the Apostle: 'Be urgent in season, out of season; reprove, entreat, rebuke with all patience and teaching' (2 Tm 4:2)."[23]

If anyone wished to write an outline of what the Church means by the priesthood, the document on the life and ministry of priests would offer an almost inexhaustible supply of material. The First Chapter (No. 2) tells us that the priest, because of his priestly ordination and sacramental differentiation from the rest of the community, works in the name of Christ for all men but in a particular and official way, fulfilling the distinctively priestly function. In No. 5, we are told that the priest alone shares in a special manner in the priesthood of Christ and that he exercises Christ's ministry when he celebrates the sacred mysteries. In No. 10, we find a reaffirmation that the priest really participates in the active priesthood of Christ, while in No. 12 we are told that because the priest is configured by the sacrament of Orders to Christ the Priest, he can exercise authority with Christ in the Church. All through this document, we find the Church in the Council teaching again and again that there *is* a distinction between the ministerial priesthood and that of all the faithful; that a priest is called out of the Christian community and empowered by a separate and unique sacrament to carry on specific functions which are the works of Christ himself.

Finally, the preface to the *Decree on the Church's Missionary Activity* sums up the Council's teaching on mission, witness, and the priesthood.

> "The Church has been divinely sent to all nations that she might be 'the universal sacrament of salvation.' Acting out of the innermost requirements of her own catholicity and in obedience to her Founder's mandate (*cf.* Mk 16:16), she strives to proclaim the gospel to all men. For the Church was founded upon the apostles, who, following in the footsteps of Christ, 'preached the message of truth and begot Churches.' Upon their successors devolves the duty of perpetuating this work through the years. Thus 'the word of God may run and be glorified' (2 Thes 3:1) and God's kingdom can be everywhere proclaimed and established."[24]

This document begins with the Father's sending his Son and teaches how we in turn share in that sending. This viewpoint, which requires that we enter into the mission of the Church, is a theologically rich and spiritually rewarding starting point; and with the Church seen as the context for all sacramental action, it is a perfect starting point for all study of the priesthood.

With this foundation, taken from the Council, the Synod began its study of the priesthood. Necessarily there was going to be a rejection of certain extravagant positions, of which I have mentioned a few in my introduction. The texts, the actual words, the plain teaching of the Council ruled out any reconciliation between such positions and Catholic teaching. But the Synod did not wish to present a negative document, merely criticizing the failure of certain theological efforts; and so it proceeded to a positive presentation of the authentic teaching of the Church.

NOTES

1. *Dogmatic Constitution on the Church,* No. 1.
2. *Ibid.,* No. 8.
3. *Ibid.,* No. 11. In this section, the Council develops the idea of sacramental participation through all seven of the sacraments.
4. *Ibid.,* No. 20. "That divine mission, entrusted by Christ to the apostles, will last until the end of the world (Mt 28:20), since the gospel which was to be handed down by them is for all time the source of all life for the Church. For this reason the apostles took care to appoint successors in this hierarchically structured society."
5. *Ibid.,* No. 8. This theme was further developed in the collective pastoral of the Bishops of the United States in commentary on the Council document, *The Church in Our Day,* The United States Catholic Conference, November 1967. "The witness of the Church to the presence of Christ in the world is a light to us and to all men of Christ's saving grace among men. That witness can only be expressed if it is seen, felt and lived in the visible Church — the evidence of Christ's incarnation in our day" (Foreword).
6. *Ibid.,* No. 10.
7. *Dogmatic Constitution on the Church,* No. 28, and *Ministry and Life of Priests,* No. 5.
8. *Ibid.*
9. *Ministry and Life of Priests,* No. 2.
10. *Dogmatic Constitution on the Church,* No. 28.
11. *Ministry and Life of Priests,* No. 2.
12. *Ibid.*
13. *Dogmatic Constitution on the Church,* No. 9.
14. *Ibid.,* No. 10. It is in this section of the Council's document that we find the now very familiar reaffirmation that the ministerial priesthood is distinct from the priesthood of all the laity "in essence not only degree."
15. *Ibid.* See Nos. 10 and 11 throughout.
16. *Ibid.,* No. 28.
17. *Ibid.* We find a reaffirmation of this same understanding of the priest's relationship with the Church in *Ministry and Life of Priests,* No. 1, and the document on priestly formation, No. 1.
18. For one interested in developing all of this in detail, there are two very fine books devoted to these points. Thanks to Father Bona-

venture Kloppenburg O.F.M., we have *Ecclesiology of Vatican II* and *The Priest.* Both works confirm what we are saying here and what is the teaching of the Council in its *Constitution on the Church.* Bonaventure Kloppenburg O.F.M., *Ecclesiology of Vatican II,* translated by Matthew O'Connell, and *The Priest: Living Instrument and Minister of Christ the Eternal Priest,* translated by Matthew O'Connell (Chicago: Franciscan Herald Press, 1974).

19. *Pastoral Constitution on the Church,* No. 40.

20. *Ibid.,* Nos. 75 and 76. "The role and competence of the Church being what it is, she must in no way be confused with the political community, nor bound to any political system. For she is at once a sign and a safeguard of the transcendence of the human person . . . The Church, founded on the Redeemer's love, contributes to the wider applications of justice and charity within and between nations. By preaching the truth of the gospel and shedding light on all areas of human activity through her teaching and the example of the faithful, she knows respect for the political freedom and responsibility of citizens and fosters these values."

21. *Decree on the Bishops' Pastoral Office,* especially No. 28.

22. *Ibid.*

23. *Decree on the Life and Ministry of Priests,* Chapters 1 and 2, especially No. 6.

24. *Decree on the Missionary Activity,* No. 1.

2. *The 1971 Synod of Bishops on the Priesthood*

SINCE THE 1971 SYNOD confirmed the Council's teaching on the priesthood, we must look at what it said. But perhaps it would be of service, since we intend to take seriously the Synod's statement, to ask what a synod is and what value its document has.

The idea of an assembly of bishops, formed in order

to assist the Pope by advice and counsel, was raised at the time of the Second Vatican Council. The Council Document *Bishops' Pastoral Office* calls such an assembly by the traditional name of a Synod and says that such an assembly would render especially helpful assistance to the Supreme Pastor of the Church.

"Bishops from various part of the world, chosen through ways and procedures established or to be established by the Roman Pontiff, will render especially helpful assistance to the supreme pastor of the Church in a council to be known by the proper name of Synod of Bishops. Since it will be acting in the name of the entire Catholic episcopate, it will at the same time demonstrate that all bishops in hierachical communion share in the responsibility for the universal Church."[1]

The Pope, at the time of the Council, made a reference to the manner in which he would receive help and support from the bishops.

"For us personally [your discussion on the episcopacy] will provide doctrinal and practical standards by which our apostolic office, endowed though it is by Christ with the fullness and sufficiency of power, may receive more help and support, in ways to be determined (*modi et rationes*) from *a more effective and responsible collaboration* with our beloved and venerable brothers in the episcopate."[2]

On September 15, 1965, the "motu proprio," *Apostolica Sollicitudo,* was promulgated.[3] By this document, synods in the Western Catholic Church were on paper revised and the newly-instituted structure was given a constitution. The importance of the document lies not only in its normative nature as an institutional guideline, but also in its theological references. Although the specific theological aspects of the nature of a Synod and its place in the Church still need to be worked out, it is becoming clear that the establishment of synods represents a further stage in the development of an ecclesiology which takes into account the principle of collegiality and the shared responsibility of bishops.

In an introduction, this "motu proprio" establishes a context for the Synod, namely, the episcopate and the doctrine of collegiality. The aims of the Synod are then listed as:

(1) To encourage close union and valued assistance between the Sovereign Pontiff and the bishops of the entire world;

(2) To insure that direct and real information is given to the Holy See on all questions involving the internal affairs of the Church and its necessary action in the world today;

(3) To facilitate agreement on essential points of doctrine and on methods of procedure in the life of the Church.[4]

The "motu proprio" stresses that the Synod is to be a consultative body, of which the chief functions will be "informing and giving advice." Nonetheless, *Apostolica Sollicitudo* does note that "It may also have deliberative power when such power is conferred upon it by the Sovereign Pontiff, who will in such cases confirm the decisions of the Synod."[5]

In this statement of the aims of the Synod, we can find some indication as to the nature of service it is to perform and also the theological standing of its statement and decisions. The Synod exists primarily to give advice and offer information; and since its members are to represent every quarter of the globe, the information offered would presumably amount to a worldwide synthesis on some specific subject. Having established such a synthesis, the bishops could offer recommendations for relevant action. This is what has actually happened in the Synods that have been held since the publication of *Apostolica Sollicitudo.* Francis X. Murphy, an established Synod watcher and writer-teacher in Rome, sees this as an institution which provides "for a continuing debate within the governing body of the Church regarding essential problems affecting its well-being and the spiritual, moral and material salvation of mankind that is the Church's main business."[6]

The Council had stressed the fact that the College of Bishops should work together, forming a unity with the Pope. By its emphasis on "collegiality," it calls attention to the dual obligation of each bishop: he is charged with the care of one diocese, and yet shares with all other bishops a concern and responsibility for the whole Church. The Synod offers an instrument through which this concern and responsibility can be channeled into practical efforts.

The First Synod met on September 29, 1967, to discuss the problems presented to it by the Holy Father: the Revision of Canon Law, the Question of Doctrine, Seminaries, Mixed Marriages, and Liturgy. Its objective, in the words of Pope Paul at the first session, was "the preservation and strengthening of the Catholic faith, its integrity, its force, its development, its doctrinal and historical coherence."[7] The Synod closed after a month of deliberation on October 29, 1967.

The second Synod — described as "an extraordinary session" — met from October 11 to October 28, 1969, to discuss the wider participation by the bishops with the Pope and each other in the government of the Church.

In each of these first two instances, the gathered Synodal Fathers conceived their work to consist in expressing their views on the proposed agenda and offering some concrete suggestions about the questions under discussion. The Holy Father's talk at the opening Mass of the first Synod reinforced this view of the Synod. It is to offer, in the Pope's words, "wider and more systematic cooperation and counsel."[8]

The Third Synod will be discussed throughout this book. The Fourth Synod — on Evangelization — began September 28 and ended October 28, 1974. Its practical value, as described by some of the American delegates there, was that it gave opportunities for the widest possible exchange of ideas. The Holy Father in his closing talk noted that the Synod had in its studies on evangelization reached many positive conclusions, even though its final statement left room for some negative reaction.[9]

Against this background of recent events, we can try to determine the theological value of a synodal document. According to the constitution set forth in *Apostolica Sollicitudo,* such a document is not a binding piece of ecclesiastical legislation. However, as an expression of the "counsel" of the College of Bishops, enhanced by their teaching authority, it is a distinctive statement of the Church's thought about some specific question. Like the reflections of a good theologian, the statements of a Synod are the result of deep penetration into the mystery of the Church in her doctrine and daily life. Like any other statement of a gathering of bishops, it reflects the pastoral care and concern of those who are the official teachers of the faith. What gives this particular form of teaching a special degree of importance is its universality. The synod does not consist of a few specialized minds addressing some problem that touches all the Church; it is rather a representative body of the whole Church facing a specific problem. Therefore, in theory, a synod should yield statements that come near to expressing a consensus of the whole magisterium, on some particular question at a given time.

And so, just as the Fathers of the Church are revered for having reflected the thinking of the Church in their own day, so in a sense the present-day Synodal Fathers reflect the thinking of the present-day Church on any selected issue. Their findings should be of great importance for theologians, teachers and faithful: they represent the teaching Church at work, and hence — for the believer — they have at least a general presumption of authority. It can of course be argued that no precisely defined theological "note" attaches to any paper of any synod. But given Catholic doctrine about the Church and about the teaching and witnessing role of the bishops within the Church, there is a very heavy presumption in favor of what they say; and a synod adds further weight to their ordinary manner of teaching, since the whole episcopate is there assembled through its representatives and speaks collectively.

The procedure is not an altogether new one. Collective pastoral letters on the part of national hierarchies have long been used to express the thinking and teaching of a country's bishops. Within the United States, the use of collective pastoral letters to explain the Council documents and apply them to the needs of a particular people was begun in 1966 with the collective pastoral letter "The Church in Our Day," 1967. The synod develops this procedure at the level of the Universal Church. But it does so with one great qualification. Any document it produces is not in itself a teaching instrument, it is merely presented to the Pope to show the thinking of the bishops of the world on a given question.

The confirmation of a synodal document by the Pope

still does not make it into a magisterial teaching document. But it does indicate that the Holy Father "accepts and confirms" the conclusions of the bishop, his prestige being added to that of their consensus. The result is therefore a weighty statement of consensus within a representative body of the Universal Church, under its Supreme Pastor.

In this sense, it needs to be taken as a serious statement — one that reflects the whole Church's thought. It is more than an exercise in mere theologizing, even though it may be less than the act of a bishop when formally teaching his people. It certainly deserves the benefit of any doubt which arises concerning the authentic teaching of the Church, and in this limited sense one can call the teaching of a synod normative. It represents a collective effort to express the teaching of the Church on a specific issue, on the part of those men who are appointed as the Church's official teachers.

The Third Synod was called to meet in Rome on September 30, 1971. It was made up of 212 delegates. One hundred and forty of them were elected by episcopal conferences; thirty were appointed by Pope Paul, the rest were delegates either "ex-officio" or by other election (representatives of religious orders). Two priest-auditors from various countries were invited by the Pope to attend plenary sessions and to participate in language-group discussions with the bishops.

The Synod's agenda included two subjects: the Priesthood, and Justice and Peace. The first act was the Mass concelebrated by Pope Paul in the Sistine Chapel. The presence of, and explicit references to, Cardinal Mindszenty, Primate of Hungary, at that Mass caused much comment. To many observers of the Synod, his presence in the midst of the Fathers seemed, in symbolic fashion, to indicate the Holy Father's views on the nature of the ministerial priesthood and its call to self-giving. This was developed even further by the beatification of Father Kolbe, who voluntarily gave up his life in a Nazi concentration camp in order that another might live. It was in this sense, at least, that many writers interpreted the Pope's opening address. The Synod was charged at that same Mass to present its views on the work and nature of the priest.

Under the presidency of Cardinals Leo Stephen Duval, John Joseph Wright, and Paul Muñoz Vega, the discussion began on the following day. On October 1, in the new hall designed expressly for such uses, the first working session was called to order.

The bishops had before them the working paper prepared by the Synod Office in active collaboration with episcopal conferences all over the world. The discussion lasted three weeks. The final summary document, worked and re-worked, was finally released under the date of November 5. It was sustained by a nearly unanimous vote of the Fathers in the final secret ballot.[10]

The text of the Synod's document on the ministerial priesthood passed through several stages of evolution before it was published in final form at the direction of the Holy Father on November 30, 1971. The document began as a tentative text that was sent to all the world's national conferences, "as preparatory material for debate."[11] The text was sent from the permanently established Synod Office at the Vatican under the direction of the Polish Bishop Ladislaus Rubin. The "schema" on the ministerial priesthood defines itself in its introduction:

"The following pages, which are being sent to the bishops, are not meant as a 'schema' which the Synod will be asked to approve and which would then be published. It is rather something to work with, something to start debate, and something from which some proposals for the Pope might come. Therefore, if some proposals are put forth in the text, they are made only as suggestions."[12]

The propositions on the ministerial priesthood attached to the text in summary form attempt to give a framework for the discussion that the document calls for. Most of these propositions had their origin in the International Theological Commission. The document, in outline form, is divided into three sections: (1) revelation, as the source of "the reality of priestly ministry"; (2) the priesthood of Christ in its nature and function; and (3) the practical implications of such a priesthood. The document left all the practical considerations for a later part, as they were to be discussed only in the light of specific doctrinal statements and clarification.

The text compiled by the Synod Office was sent to the episcopal conferences of the world with the request that recommendations concerning it be returned to that office. Each conference was free to select its own manner of studying and making recommendations.

The working text given the Synodal Fathers when they gathered on October 1, 1971, was compiled by taking the suggested recommendations, as received by the Synod Office, and inserting them into the original text so as to form a new paper. This paper was presented to the Fathers by Cardinal Höffner, who — as a member of the pre-synodal commission — was partly responsible for its preparation. To handle the material sent to the Synod Office as suggestions following the "schema," two commissions were established. One, under Cardinal Joseph Höffner, Archbishop of Köln, was charged with the preparation of the Doctrinal Part of the paper. The special secretary to this commission was Msgr. Jorge Medina Estévez of the Catholic University of Santiago in Chile. Cardinal Vincent Enrique y Taracón, Archbishop of Toledo, was the relator of the Practical Part of the paper. Working with him as special Secretary was Msgr. Albert Bovone of the Vatican Congregation for the Clergy.

The text given the Synod as a working paper began by speaking of the Church as the focal point or *"locus"* of the priesthood. It also indicated that the doctrinal statement would have to consider the priesthood with reference to the Church's nature as the community of faith and the sacraments. "It is impossible to analyze the priestly ministry without reflecting at the same time on the mystery of the Church . . ." "The priestly ministry has its place at the center of the community and presupposes the existence of a community spirit."[13]

In emphasizing the sacramental context of the priesthood and the specifically sacramental role of the priest, the Synod's first working document seems to choose sacramental function as its starting point. Evangelical function (specifically as witness), is only mentioned later in the paper, as a corollary to the sacramental office.

Archbishop Plourde of Ottawa, commenting on the working paper, noted that two models could be used in thinking about the Church. The first followed the scheme Christ-Apostles-Hierarchy-Church; the second followed the order Christ-Church-Ministries.[14] The outline of the working paper clearly followed the first pattern. But the debate within the Synod gradually produced a text with an order that combined both of the schemes listed by Plourde.

The working paper summed up the doctrine of the ministerial priesthood in ten statements:

1. Christ founded his Church by means of his priestly action.
2. Christ gave the Church the task of keeping present the work of redemption until his return: the Church is therefore essentially sacerdotal.
3. In order to be able to accomplish her mission, the Church was provided by Christ with a variety of gifts and ministries.
4. According to the doctrine of Vatican Council II, the priestly ministry is based on "divine institution" and endowed with "sacred power."
5. Even if one were to recognize in the primitive Church a certain development of structures, the priestly ministry retains its substantial identity.
6. The ecclesiastical ministry instituted by God is exercised in different orders — those called from earliest antiquity episcopal, presbyterial, and diaconal.
7. The priestly ministry is conferred through the communication of the Holy Spirit, that is, through the sacrament of ordination.
8. Priestly ordination is not an inefficacious sign: it is a dynamic force that embraces the whole life of the priest who is dedicated to the service of God and men; it pervades his whole person.
9. The annunciation of the gospel, the administration of the sacraments, and the celebration of the Eucharistic Mystery have a mutual relationship to each other, and in their intimate connection they constitute one single priestly service for the building up of Christ's mystical body.
10. The ministerial priesthood, even though it is for the service of the kingdom of God, which is not of this

world, has and must of necessity have consequences for the temporal order.

The narrow concentration on the sacramental aspects of the priestly ministry found in this outline was eventually to give way to a wider perspective as we shall see when we come to the final document.

The next step in the development of the text was the discussion by the Synod of the "working paper." The work began October 1, with nine of the Fathers speaking on behalf of their respective episcopal conferences. The discussion lasted through seven meetings, at which eighty-two cardinals, patriarchs, archbishops, bishops and religious superiors spoke. All these recommendations and modifications were presented to the chairman, to be used by the Special Commission when revising the document for a further presentation to the Fathers.

Cardinal Höffner's commission then prepared a wide-ranging synthesis of the debate. Working on the interventions already made, the Cardinal was able to give to the Fathers, as an outline for discussion, the principal points raised in the general meeting.

In his summary, Cardinal Höffner pointed out that two approaches to the ministerial priesthood had been proposed. One would begin from the unshakable doctrine of the ministerial office; the other would begin from present problems.[15]

To permit a more detailed study of the text and the interventions, the general assembly of the Synod was divided into smaller working groups, each having a common language. It was the purpose of each language group to prepare a *Relatio* for the general assembly, based on the particular understanding by the members of the group of the problems and solutions facing the

Synod in the light of the interventions and the discussions within the group.[16]

The material available to the Fathers as they approached the smaller groups for the discussion on the final text was enormous. Many national hierarchies had prepared studies on the priesthood; some individual bishops had initiated local studies on the nature and function of the priesthood and had introduced these at the language-group meetings. The United States Bishops had had prepared a study entitled *American Priests,* a Report of the National Opinion Research Center (University of Chicago Press; Chicago, 1971); they also had their own report on the priesthood, prepared by a special group of theologians at the request of the National Conference of Catholic Bishops,[17] and the "Report of the Regional Meetings on the Ministerial Priesthood."[18]

The division of views on the methodology to be used in drawing up the text was found again in the language-group reports and in the discussion and preparation of the final text. The question was: should the text begin with a set of doctrinal statements and work for an application of these to specific problems confronting the Church today? — or should the document begin with the problems facing the Church and work toward an understanding of the priesthood in the light of the problems?

The original working paper — the one presented to the Synod on October 1 — favored the first approach, beginning with a doctrinal statement. As we have seen, it began with doctrinal propositions and reserved practical questions until nearly the end. This was explained in the paper itself, where it was said that certain popular opinions about the ministerial priesthood distort Catholic doctrine. The first need, therefore, is for a positive doctrinal statement on the subject.[19]

Bishop William Baum's intervention reflected a position that is found in the final text. He called for a statement of doctrine on the priesthood to clarify any doubt that might exist while still leaving the door open for further theological development.[20]

The alternative view to that found in Cardinal Höffner's outline was voiced from the floor and in the language-group meetings. That position is best represented in the intervention of the French language Group B under Father Lecuyer. It was the opinion of this group that doctrine should not be presented in abstract formulae but in the context of the difficulties that priests encounter today.[21]

John Hogan in *The Irish Times* saw the opinion on this point as divided into three viewpoints. The first group's position is summed up as "If the Synod did not make a clear statement in line with what had been taught by the Second Vatican Council, it would be judged by history."

"The second group is anxious to deal with immediate, practical problems and attempts to steer the Synod away from making any statement which would terminate or constrict legitimate theological discussion about the priesthood. This group includes Cardinal Suenens, Bishop Weber of Graz, Austria, Father Joseph Lecuyer, Superior General of the Congregation of the Holy Spirit, and Archbishop McGrath of Panama.

"Thirdly, there is a small group of Eastern Rite prelates who stress the particular experiences of their own Churches."[22]

On Thursday, October 7, Cardinal Taracón presented to the Synod the text of the second section of the document — the one dealing with the Practical Problems of the Ministerial Priesthood. While the morning sessions of the Synod turned its attention to the second section of the document, the afternoon sessions were still devoted to discuss in depth the doctrinal part of the document.

After all the reports of the various language groups had been presented, the reports were turned over to the Synod's Commission which had the task of writing the text to be presented for final approval. The draft sent to the Fathers for their vote and approval underwent one final re-writing as a result of their voting. The text was submitted to a section-by-section vote, which permitted the Fathers to indicate any particular areas with which they were still not completely satisfied. The document was then forwarded to the Holy Father.

In a rescript dated November 30, 1971, of an audience given by the Holy Father to the Cardinal Secretary of State, it states that,

"His Holiness now accepts and confirms all the conclusions in the two documents."[23]

NOTES

1. *Decree on Bishops' Pastoral Office in the Church,* No. 5.
2. Xavier Rynn, *The Second Session* (New York: Farrar Straus, 1964), p. 355.
3. AAS, Vol. LVII, No. 775. For a complete English translation of the "Motu Proprio," see "Canon Law Digest," T.L. Bouscaren and James T. O'Connor (Milwaukee: Bruce, Supplement 1965).
4. AAS LVII, 775 seq.
5. AAS LVII 776: "Poterit etiam potestate deliberativa gaudere ubi haec ei collata fuerit a Romano Pontifice, cuius erit in hoc casu decisiones Synodi ratas habere."
6. Francis X. Murphy, Synod '67: *A New Sound in Rome* (Milwaukee: Bruce, 1968), p. 10.
7. AAS LIX, 963.
8. AAS LIX, 967: "atque etiam apertior et potior Nobis visa est necessitas modo ampliore et magis disposito utendi auxiliatrice opera

et consilio Fratrum Nostrorum in Episcopatu ad pastoralem moderationem ipsius Ecclesiae."

9. Origins, N C Documentary Service, Vol. 4, No. 20, p. 310.

10. The first text sent to all the Episcopal Conferences was entitled "De Sacerdotio Ministeriali" (Lineamenta Argumentorum de Quibus Disceptabitur in Secundo Coetu Generali). This text in English is found in the "Documentary Service" Press Service, United States Catholic Conference, April 29, 1971. The text presented to the Bishops on their arrival at the Synod meeting is found in English in "L'Osservatore Romano," English Edition, No. 41 (185), October 14, 1971, p. 5. It bears, as do nearly all of the preparatory papers of the Synod, the title, "De Sacerdotio Ministeriali."

The material connected with the Synod that bears the title "De Sacerdotio Ministeriali" is as follows:

a. "De Sacerdotio Ministeriali Lineamenta Argumentorum de Quibus Disceptabitur in Secondo Coetu Generali." This is the document sent to the hierarchies around the world as a "working paper" or "schema." When quoted, its full title will be given.

b. "De Sacerdotio Ministeriali, Relatio, de Parte Doctrinali." This is the document that Cardinal Höffner introduced to the assembled Synodal Fathers at the opening of the Synod. It was to be the paper that was to be the basis for discussion and represented the amalgamation of the "working paper" and the replies of the bishops of the world. When quoted, it will be so as "De Sacerdotio Ministeriali," Relatio.

c. "De Sacerdotio Ministeriali, Relatio Post Disceptationem, de Parte Doctrinali." This is the paper that Cardinal Höffner presented to the Synod as the summary of the interventions and remarks of the Synodal Fathers. It superseded "b" in the preparation of the final text.

d. "De Sacerdotio Ministeriali." This is the final text which was released as the work of the Synod on November 5, 1971, but was not published in final form with the Holy Father's approbation until November 30, 1971 (AAS, Vol. LXIII, No. 1971, p. 898). This text was given in five modern languages as well as the Latin. We will quote from the English. The English title is "The Ministerial Priesthood."

11. N.C. News Service, "Documentary Service," Introduction, p. 1.

12. *Ibid.*

13. De Sacerdotio Ministeriali, Relatio, De Parte Doctrinali, Typis Polyglottis Vaticanis, MCMLXXI, p. 6, Quarto.

14. "Tablet," Vol. 225, No. 6855, p. 1034.

15. In the actual count of suggestions, the Fathers overwhelmingly supported, according to the speech of Cardinal Höffner, the need to

start with some fixed doctrinal statements.

"Longe maior pars interventum priori methodo (a fundamentis immutabilibus muneris ministerialis in Ecclesia) favet spe ducta fore ut exhinc ad securas conclusiones practicas pervenire possimus." "De Sacerdotio Ministeriali," Relatio post Disceptationem, De Parte Doctrinali, Typis Polyglottis Vaticanis, MCMLXXI, p. 6 (unpublished).

16. The groups were classified according to language and were as follows:

Latin:
Moderator Cardinal Felici, Relator Patriarch Batanian

French:
"A" Moderator Cardinal Garrone, Relator Archbishop Etchegaray
"B" Moderator Cardinal Marty, Relator Father Lecuyer
"C" Moderator Cardinal Suenens, Relator Bishop Schmitt

German:
Moderator Cardinal Doepfner, Relator Bishop Hengsbach

English:
"A" Moderator Cardinal Conway, Relator Archbishop Cordeiro
"B" Moderator Cardinal Dearden, Relator Father Heston
"C" Moderator Cardinal Carberry, Relator Father van Asten

Spanish-Portuguese:
"A" Moderator Archbishop Brandao Vilela, Relator Bishop Derisi
"B" Moderator Cardinal Landazuri Ricketts, Relator Archbishop McGrath
"C" Moderator Archbishop Pironio, Relator Bishop Torres Oliver.

17. "Report of the Subcommittee on the Systematic Theology of the Priesthood," Committee on Priestly Life and Ministry of the National Conference of Catholic Bishops, NCCB, Washington, D.C., 1971.

18. Documentation for the General Meeting of the National Conference of Catholic Bishops, April 17–19, 1971, Detroit. For a more complete listing of this material, see the bibliography of this paper, also International Documentation on the Contemporary Church (IDOC), "Catalogue of Documents Supplement N. 1, Synod of Bishops," Rome, October, 1971.

19. "Nemo ignorat hodie non raro opiniones doctrinam Ecclesiae de sacerdotio ministeriali depravantes proferri." "De Sacerdotio Ministeriali," Relatio, p. 6.

20. Bishop William Baum, Bishop of Springfield-Cape Girardeau, Intervention, p. 1 (unpublished).

21. "Ne suffragium instituatur super partem doctrinalem antequam etiam conclusiones practicae suffragio proponantur . . . tandem ne suffragium feratur super intergrum quoddam schema sed super propositiones particulares." "De Parte Doctrinali, Schematis De Min-

isterio Sacerdotali, Relatio Circuli Gallici b." (unpublished).

22. "Tablet," October 9, pp. 988-89.

23. "Sanctitas Sua iam nunc probat atque confirmat omnes conclusiones, quae in praedictis documentis cum vigentibus normis congruunt," AAS, Vol. LXIII, No. 1971, 898.

3. *The Church*

THE FOCAL POINT of the priesthood is Christ. The Church is the extension in time and space of the Incarnate Lord. It therefore is the context of all witness-mission. It is Christ's mission that the Church carries on. She is therefore the foremost means instituted by God to pass on his self-revelation.

"The Church . . . was established to be a sacrament of the salvation which came to us from God in Christ. In her, Christ is present and operative for the world as a Savior . . ."[1]

As the extension in time and space of the risen and ascended Christ, the Church uniquely participates in and parallels the Incarnation. It participates in the Incarnation to the extent that its identification with Christ is able to be expressed only through human and visible means. It parallels the Incarnation in its practical, functional relationship to the revelation of the Father to the world. To the Church is given the full office of testifying to all the works of God. In this sense the Church can claim to be the only witness to Christ. She was created to be Christ's extension in the world. Her members share his life, his function in their faith. Yet their role is mediated by the Church. Only in and through it can they authentically and fully witness Christ. As the Church is the first to participate in Christ's redemptive action in the world, so does each believer through his membership in the Church participate in the same mission. But the individual makes this claim to witness specifically as a member of the Church. His mission is received through her. All of this was summed up (the Synod believed) by Tertullian: "The Church from the apostles, the apostles from Christ, Christ from God."

The quotation from Tertullian, the *Praesci. Haer.* XXI, 4, found in I, 3, 1, confirms the Synod's ecclesial-centered view of redemption. This understanding of the Christian experience was not unique among the Patristic writers. St. John Chrysostom centers the entire salvific work of Christ in the Church; first in the apostles and then in those called in the manner of the apostles by ordination:

"Our Lord was not content with merely encouraging his apostles by calling their ministry a harvest. He went farther and strengthened them by giving them power to reap this harvest," *Homily 32* on St. Matthew, No. 3; P.G. Vol. 5 C. 380.

Then, speaking of this power which he confirms is transmitted in ordination, he writes of the imposition of hands:

"By this means spiritual benefits are transmitted . . . and the priest receives the ministry of the Word," *Homily 14* on the Acts, No. 3; P.G. Vol. 60. C. 116.

In this specification of witness we can see another affirmation of the Synod's view of the Church as the principal manifestation of Christ in the world. All functions of priesthood, witness, and community building must be seen in the context of the Church. They are valid only as they participate in the Church's carrying out of her mission.

The logic of Tertullian's remark is followed through in the document. All begins from God in Christ. Christ is found in his apostles. The Church today carries on the office and ministry of the apostles.[2]

The primacy of the collective witness of the community does not in any way minimize the witness value of each member. The nature of witness requires that it be specifically personal. But at the same time it must be part of a larger context. The personal witness of the believer is thus able to impart the truth — the faith.

By explaining witness in this manner, the document also settles the question of the authenticity of individual witness. Each priest is called to be a witness of the faith. His testimony is to be the instrument that leads others to the life of the faith and confirms those already living it. But individual witness must be valid. Authentic witness must be related to the Church and identified with her mission, for both participate in the same mediation and witness of Christ. As Christ is the unique witness of the Father and the Church, the divinely-appointed one of

Christ, so the individual priest is a witness to revelation. He participates as does the Church in the revealing action of Christ but precisely as a member of the Church. His witness is valid only in the context of the principal testimony given by the Church. He shares in the Church's ministry of testimony and office of witness only as he is in communion with her. This unity necessarily pertains to the doctrine taught and the faith handed down. As to the continuation of Christ's witness and the verification of the testimony concerning Christ himself, the Church is the first and complete witness to God and the *force* of his mediation in the world today. The witness of an individual to the truth of the faith can never be independent of the witness of the Church. Both speak of what they have — not of themselves — but of another.

But in respect of the ordained priest, the idea of witness is subject to a further modification. As a consecrated sharer of the mission of the apostles through the Church, the priest shares in the magisterial action of the Church, which is in itself an authoritative teaching action. The priest's activity as a witness, therefore, becomes the work of an official authoritative witness. This is touched on in the first section of the Second Part of the Synod's document. However, the full import of its teaching can only be seen in the light of the document *Ministry and Life of Priests.* The Council document quoted by the Synod at this point of its development shows in greater detail the relationship between authentic priestly witness and ministerial ordination.[3]

"The People of God finds its unity first of all through the Word of the living God, which is quite properly sought from the lips of priests. Since no one can be saved who has not first believed, priests, as co-workers with their bishops, have as their primary duty the proclamation of the gospel of God to all.

"Thus the ministry of the Word is carried out in many ways, according to the various needs of those who hear and the special gifts of those who preach. In areas or communities which are non-Christian, the gospel message draws men to faith and the sacraments of salvation. In the Christian community itself, especially among those who seem to understand or believe little of what they practice, the preaching of the Word is needed for the very administration of the sacraments. For these are sacraments of faith, and faith is born of the Word and nourished by it."[4]

The Synod notes the Church's obligation to maintain the continuity of the faith from age to age. For continuity is of the essence of witness.[5] It essentially relies on continuity between the fact witnessed and the testimony of it. Continuity is absolutely essential to authentic and credible witness. And only in union with the Church can the individual find continuity. His witness as it shares in the testimony of the Church can lay claim to the continuity of the living witness of the Church only as he is in communion and conformity with the Faith as the Church believes and receives it.

Saint Paul in his First Epistle to the Corinthians argues the authenticity of his testimony in terms of what the apostles believe and, therefore, its continuity with what the whole Church believes. In the Acts, to safeguard the testimony of the Church and insure its historicity and credibility, it was insisted that the number of apostles, diminished by Judas' death, be filled only by "one of those who bore us company all the while we had the Lord Jesus with us, coming and going, from John's ministry of baptism until the day when he was taken from us — one of those must now join us as a witness to his Resurrection" (Acts 2:2).

The individual witness participates in the witness that is the Church. He, therefore, shares in her continuity and her infallibility, while and because he is joined to her. All the authenticity in his testimony depends on the relationship he maintains to that same Church. For as the witness to Christ and God's mighty works, the Church is the first and only witness. All individuals share in this work as members of the Church, and should always be humble before her greater witness To the teaching Church is entrusted the obligation of spreading the faith, of passing on the saving word. She must bear witness to the presence of God and to our life in him. If any man is to be saved by his participation in the saving action of Christ, if he is to be counted as one who "knows Christ" and so has faith in him and possesses eternal life, then he must know of that supernatural reality that is Christ and his redemptive plan. Each one must be given an opportunity to hear of that truth, to have it witnessed before him, to have its reality testified in his presence. This is the function of the witnessing, teaching Church in the person of the priest.

The Synod document notes a differentiation within the Christian community not only in terms of sacramental ministry but also in terms of the protection of the integrity of the Church's witness. Not only are some men called to serve the Church in specifically ministerial actions, but they are entrusted with the integrity of the gospel message. In this the Synod again links the office of official teacher in the Church with the office of ministerial priesthood and sees *their* function as divinely commissioned.

The development of this line of thought leads us to another affirmation found in the Synod's reasoning. The Church's witness is a witness to specific doctrines and events.

The witness of the Church is not a vague hope or a

groundless euphoria. It is a clear testimony to precise events, a judgment articulated about certain facts and a specific person, Jesus of Nazareth. And like any society, the Church has certain specific members who speak for it. Obviously, the Church, as an organic whole, cannot testify. Her spokesmen do. Within the Church are those teachers, successors to the apostles, called bishops. Of their functions in the Church, one primary duty is that of official witness or spokesman for the incarnate witness that is the living Church. The bishop for the local Church and all bishops for the universal Church, always with Peter as their head, bear the ministry of witness in a particular manner. Again, here we are speaking of witness in relation to the faith as creed. As the official ministers of testimony to the truth, the bishops are the first to discharge the Church's duty as appointed witness. Specifically, the bishop is a teacher, one set apart from the Church to teach both within its confines and to those not yet of its brotherhood. His primary function as successor to the apostles is that of witness to all that Jesus has said and done. He, therefore, is the first witness in the particular or local church.

All individual testimony to the truth revealed in Christ Jesus must find its touchstone of authenticity in relation to that voiced — given flesh in words — by the Church through her official witness. This does not mean that witness within the Church is limited to only the bishop: the obligation to bear testimony concerning all that Jesus said and did falls upon every believer. But in that body of believers — gifted with various talents, gifts, callings and ministries — there are those chosen specifically to see that the common witness is never lost, confused or misunderstood. The office of official, authentic witness becomes necessary in a Church that is incarnate in a world not yet perfect. It corresponds to the obvious and deep need of any society for authentic spokesmen for the values that establish and maintain it. Teaching authority in the Church exercises a function that represents the community's awareness of itself and its belief about itself. It is in one aspect the community's self-expression of its faith as received and believed. Authority implies that someone has been appointed to speak for the whole. Within the Church, also a community of men, that same need is necessarily felt; and the answer to it lies in the structure of that same community, as expressed in the days of its foundation.

The Synod, like Saint Paul, uses the analogy of the human body to express the notion that within the Church there are various functions, roles and gifts. Within the Church, the bishops, successors to the apostles, function as official witnesses to the works of God. The Synod reaffirms the teaching of the Church that the bishops have special prerogatives in relation to the maintenance of the continuity of the faith and, therefore, to the authenticity of the witness given in its regard. And since each priest shares in the mission of the bishop, he must also participate in this specifically authentic witness that is the office of the bishop.

It is clear that the document of the Synod stresses the role of the priest as witness. He has an indispensable work which consists in carrying on the initial revelation of Christ. As a witness, the priest is to pass on to others, in word and deed, the news that he has received. Priestly witness is made within the Church. Such witness participates in the authenticity of the Church's witness because the priest shares in the call of the Church through the bishop to spread the message. The guarantee of truth rests in the continuity that the witness maintains with the teaching Church. This follows on the assertion that the priest — because of his calling and his participation in the official teaching duty of the Church — is a minister of witness. His ministry, as seen in this document, consists in the authentic extension of the word of God through the participation in the witness of Christ made present in the Church.

NOTES

1. I, 3.
2. *Ibid.*
3. II, 1.
4. "Ministry and Life of Priests," No. 4.
5. Seen in the context of specifically priestly functions, the priesthood's continuity is traced by the Synod back to the apostles (1, 4). The need of the priesthood in maintaining the Church's fidelity and visible continuity with the apostolic tradition is seen by the Synod in the wider context of hierarchical structure and communion (I, 4). Hans Küng, *Why Priests?*, sees the wider context of the Church as the sole foundation of the continuity of priestly and episcopal orders. ". . . the apostolic mission and service were assumed by the Church as a whole, which, as a whole, can and should remain the 'Ecclesia apostolica,' " p. 33. This point we shall discuss in a later chapter.

4. *The Mission of Christ*

WITNESS OR THE bearing of testimony is the priest's function. It is the concrete extension of Christ's mission. As Christ is a teacher, witness, and means of salvation, so also is the priest. The source of all sacerdotal action is Christ. The priest is not a second-hand reflection of what the Lord was nor is what he does an imitation of Christ's work. Rather, through the priest, the Lord continues his own work and mission here and now.

The priest is differentiated from all other members of the Church precisely by the way in which he is identified with Christ's one unique saving work. The Church has always noted that certain powers are reserved for specific members who share in a unique way in Christ's mission. Saint Paul certainly was conscious that he acted by Christ's mission and mandate. In the New Testament we see this mission being passed on with the solemn obligation that it be handed on to generations yet to come. We even find a solemn warning: "Do not be too quick to lay hands on any man" (I Tm 5: 23). The two Epistles to Timothy and the Epistle to Titus express the sacramental aspects of the laying on of hands, and they point out that ordination is not just a calling to a type of community service but a real and fearful consecration.

The Synod's document offers several affirmations on the nature of the priesthood. These affirmations grow out of two principles which it repeats insistently. The first is that the mission of the priest is identical with that of Christ. In the section entitled "Origin and Nature of the Hierarchical Ministry" we find that it is "the priestly ministery of the New Testament which continues Christ's function as mediator and alone perpetuates the essential work . . ."[1]

The patristic roots of this argument run deep. Examples are found in some detail in St. John Chrysostom and even more explicitly in St. Leo:

"No one can say that after receiving the imposition of hands I have been wanting in my duty. Nevertheless this is not my doing but the work of Christ." St. John, *Homily 29 on the Epistle to the Romans,* P. G. Vol. 60. c. 656.

"Consequently, it is not with bold presumption that, while mindful of divine goodness, we honor the day on which we accepted the office of high priest. We confess in all gratitude and truth that in whatever good we may do in the exercise of our ministry it is Christ himself who works in us." St. Leo, *Sermo,* 5, "In Natali Ipsius," P.L. Vol. 54, c. 154.

The second principle is that the essential notes which demonstrate Christ's priestly nature are seen in Christ's actual work and accomplishment. The entire force of the opening paragraphs "Christ, Alpha and Omega" is that Christ in his actions "performed," "signified," and "manifested" his priesthood. Jesus was "sanctified" and "sent," "marked with the seal." He "proclaimed," "preached," "confirmed by signs," "laid down his life," "rose from the dead," "reconciled," "laid the foundation of the people of the new covenant." All of this action is continued in the Church. "In her, Christ is present and operative for the world as a saviour." The priest carries on in this work and therefore expresses the priesthood as Christ's work does. "The priestly ministry . . . continues Christ's function . . . and perpetuates" his action.[2]

In this the Synod follows the general order of the Council's treatment of the priesthood. The document *Ministry and Life of Priests* "takes as its perspective the uniqueness and unity of the priestly consecration and mission of Christ."[3] St. John Chrysostom saw this unity in terms of the mediatorship that is both Christ's and the priest's. He bases all his specifications of distinctively sacerdotal holiness on the priest's character as mediator (*On the Priesthood,* Bk. 6, P.G. Vol. 48 c. 680).

The same point is made explicitly in the original schema of the Synod

"A Christian who is ordained for priestly ministry . . . shares in his own way in the priesthood of Christ; he represents Christ, who is the head of the community, in that community and before its eyes . . . This means that the exercise of priestly ministry in preaching the gospel, in forgiving sins, in celebrating the Eucharist, etc., is not a simple function or a community exercise . . . ; rather it requires a true *consecration,* a true *mission,* perpetually joined with the consecration and mission of the apostles . . . Every priest fulfills the role of Christ in his own way (*Ministry and Life of Priests,* N. 12) by participating in the mission which the risen Christ gave to his apostles."[4]

The final document says the same thing more concisely, and also brings in the sense of this paragraph from the Council document, *Ministry and Life of Priests*: "By the laying on of hands there is communicated a gift of the Holy Spirit which cannot be lost. This readily configures the ordained minister to Christ, consecrates him and makes him a sharer in Christ's mission."[5]

Instead of beginning with a detailed outline of the nature of the priesthood as seen in itself, the document prefers to begin with the work that Christ performed, in order to ascertain from this the nature of the priestly mission. As the priest is identified with Christ's work, so he must in the accomplishment of that work be identified with Christ.

The specific character of this line of thought is that it located the area of study of the identity of a priest in the mission he shares with Christ. The priest does a certain work which is unique in that it shares in Christ's work which is properly His own. The study of the priesthood begins, for the Synod, in the understanding of that work which the priest shares with Christ. It does not say that the priest is only a priest when he functions as one. But it does say that in the priestly action of Christ we can see the elements that constitute the priesthood. In this sense we can say that the document places heavy emphasis on the witness/mission aspect of priestly ministry. For the priest carries on the mission of Christ and finds in that mission his own identity.

We find an outline to this approach to the discussion of the essence of the priesthood (in terms of the work that Christ did) in some of the reports that were prepared by the various language groups. The German-language group under Bishop Hengsbach emphasized the understanding of the priesthood in terms of Christ's activities.

"Exegesis does not tell us much about the person of Christ . . . but the priest should follow Christ in whose name he acts."[6]

"From the gospel and the Acts of the Apostles, one sees the stress placed on the pastoral function. This consists in the preaching of the gospel, the uniting and governing of the ecclesiastical community, the forgiveness of sins and above all the celebration of the Eucharist over which the priest alone may preside by virtue of his ordination."[7]

The language-group reports emphasize the actions of Christ in which the priest participates as the starting point in defining the priesthood.[8]

The delineation of the priestly work of Christ is important to the understanding of the Synod's view of the priesthood. For up to this point the document has spoken of the context of the priesthood, i.e., the Church, its hierarchical nature, the derived nature of the priesthood, and the role of the bishop within the Church. Now the Synod's attention turns to the essential characteristics of the priesthood, which are noted only as they are found in Christ. The basis for this statement is the theological principle indicated by many Synodal Fathers and set forth very clearly in the intervention of Archbishop Farah.

"The ministerial priesthood consists essentially in the participation in the eternal priesthood of Christ."[9]

The sentence sums up what the document expressed in more developed terms. The ministerial priesthood shares in the priesthood of Christ. The sharing in Christ's priesthood constitutes the essence of the ministerial priesthood. But the priesthood of Christ is seen only in his works of salvation and redemption. So, too, the essence of the ministerial priesthood must be seen in the works of Christ in which the priest shares.

Farah's intervention goes on to see this as the necessary result of the Incarnation. Human limitations required the Incarnation. So human limitations hinder the definition of the priesthood except in terms of its function. But the text of the quote goes on to point out that this does not mean that the priesthood is a temporary function. The function is a constitutive one for the ministerial priesthood as it was for Christ.

"The priesthood of Christ is not solely spiritual; it consists in obedience to the law of the Incarnation. The priesthood sharing in the mystery of the Trinity can be conferred only by the Holy Spirit through men chosen by the Spirit. This conception is faithful to the oriental tradition and has its foundations in Sacred Scripture. Priesthood is not a temporary function but a definitive consecration."[10]

This intervention tries to show the link between the two approaches to the study of the priesthood. The reference to "definitive consecration" finds its way in various forms into the final document. But even here the discussion is directed to showing that priestly function is permanent, not transient.

The same affirmation is made in the recent document of the Sacred Congregation for the Doctrine of the Faith dated June 24, 1973, which cites the Synod document on the "enduring nature of the priestly character."

". . . the Second General Assembly of the Synod of Bishops rightly considered the enduring nature of the priestly character throughout life as pertaining to the teaching of the faith."[11]

In short, the Synod sees the identification of each priest with Christ, the One Priest. Whatever was Christ's priestly mission is in some way the priest's mission today. And whatever Christ was that enabled him to accomplish his mission, so is the priest to some extent.

Christ was a priest because of what he did. But that work can be said to be constitutive of Christ's priesthood only in the sense that it actualized and externalized what would otherwise have remained a hidden relationship of Jesus to the world. Only by acting in the way he did to redeem man did he manifest his priestly power. By virtue of his Incarnation, Christ was a priest. But only by redeeming man did his priesthood take on visible form and become intelligible to man. His activity, therefore, can be said to have brought his priesthood into the realm of human understanding, appreciation, and experience.

Beginning with the reality of human experience, we are able to see the activity of Christ that manifested his priestly character. The priest continues those actions and therefore must see his priesthood in terms of those redeeming events. But at the same time, the logic of this leads us to admit that whatever it was that permitted Christ to complete his priestly work must at the same time permit the priest to carry on the work. Identification with Christ cannot be completed solely in approximating his activities. For those activities depend on a specific spiritual power. For this reason, the Synod, in both instances, sees identification with Christ as the issue. In the first case, the reference is to a "definitive consecration" that unites a priest to Christ. In the latter, it designates the function that constitutes active priesthood.

In so far as any study of the elements of that priesthood are concerned, the starting point must remain that which was experienced and understood by men — the priestly action of Christ.

The Synod's text links the participation by the priest in Christ's priesthood with his unique ability to function in a specific manner.

"Among the various charisms and services, the priestly ministry of the New Testament, which continues Christ's function as mediator, and which in essence and not merely in degree is distinct from the common priesthood of all the faithful (*cf.* LG 10), alone perpetuates the essential work of the Apostles: by effectively proclaiming the gospel, by gathering together and leading the community, present in the exercise of his work of redeeming mankind and glorifying God perfectly."[12]

Again the document speaks in terms identifying the priest and Christ, in the priestly action of Christ carried on by the ordained minister.

"The priestly ministry reaches its summit in the celebration of the Eucharist, which is the source and centre of the Church's unity. Only a priest is able to act in the person of Christ in presiding over and effecting the sacrificial banquet wherein the People of God are associated with Christ's offering (cf. LG 28)."[13]

The document at this point refers to the teaching of Christ as found in the *Dogmatic Constitution on the Church* numbers 24, 27 and 28.

In the light of the Council's teaching we can see more clearly the Synod's emphasis on priestly identification with Christ in his actions. The council states:

"By his power [the Holy Spirit's] the [the apostles] were to be witnesses to Christ before the nations . . . Now that duty is a true service, and in sacred literature is significantly called 'diakonia' or ministry (*cf.* Acts 1:17, 25; 21:19; Rom 11:13; 1 Tm 1:12) (24).

"Christ, whom the Father sanctified and sent into the world (Jn 10:36) has, through his apostles, made their successors, the bishops, partakers of his consecration and his mission. These in their turn have legitimately handed on to different individuals in the Church various degrees of participation in this ministry. Thus the divinely established ecclesiastical ministry is exercised on different levels by those who from antiquity have been called bishops, priests and deacons . . . They exercise this sacred function of Christ most of all in the Eucharistic liturgy or synaxis. There, acting in the person of Christ, and proclaiming his mystery, they join the offering of the faithful to the sacrifice of their Head . . ." (28).

The document points out the logical sequence — "Christ-apostles-priests" in the same unique action of bringing redemption to the world — that is amplified in this section of the Synod's document. Where the Council states:

"They exercise this sacred function of Christ most of all in the Eucharistic liturgy or synaxis. There, acting in the person of Christ . . . they join the offering of the faithful to the sacrifice of their Head" (28),

the Synod says:

"The priestly ministry reaches its summit in the celebration of the Eucharist . . . Only a priest is able to act in the person of Christ in presiding over and effecting the sacrificial banquet . . ."[14]

The continued reliance of the Synod document upon the *Dogmatic Constitution on the Church,* which is cited nine times directly and numerous other times indirectly, helps us to understand the Synod's insistence on an ecclesial context for the priesthood. It also explains the emphasis on the mission of the Church as the context within which we must locate the works of a priest.

The declaration of the Congregation for the Doctrine of the Faith (June 24, 1973) cites the *Dogmatic Constitution on the Church* in the same context as does the Synod in reference to the priestly action centered in the Eucharistic sacrifice.

To sum up, we can say that the foundation of the Synod's theology on the priesthood is the statement that each priest functions as did Christ, in that he acts to carry on the work of Christ. In these activities of the priest that continue the priestly work of Christ, we see the identity of the priest. The "how" of this identification is not studied in this part of the document.

In explaining how the priest can function as Christ, the Synod speaks of the priesthood as an identification on the most fundamental level with Christ.

"By the laying on of hands there is communicated a gift of the Holy Spirit which cannot be lost (*cf.* 2 Tm 1:6). This reality configures the ordained minister to Christ, the Priest, consecrates him (*cf.* P.O. 2) and makes him a sharer in Christ's mission under its two aspects of authority and service.

"This special participation in Christ's priesthood does not disappear even if a priest for ecclesial or personal reasons is dispensed or removed from the exercise of his ministry."[15]

The declaration of the Congregation for the Doctrine of the Faith uses this same section and quotes from the Synod to make its point on the nature of the priesthood.

"In recent times the Second Vatican Council more than once mentioned it, and the second General Assembly of the Synod of Bishops rightly considered the enduring nature of the priestly character throughout life as pertaining to the teaching of the faith. This stable existence of a priestly character must be recognized by the faithful and has to be taken into account in order to judge properly about the nature of the priestly ministry and the appropriate ways of exercising it" (P. 17).

This bring us to the almost mystical understanding of the dignity of the priestly office, and certainly carries us into the realm of identification with Christ that the Council called "essential"[16] and classical theology referred to as "ontological."[17]

We find the theological term "character" used to indicate the identification of the priest with Christ. The scriptural foundation for the doctrine of sacramental character is the "seal" (*sphragis*) of God with which the elect are marked (Rv 7:2-9).[18]

The identification of the priest with Christ in a complete, mystical, and functional way is the theme of many works of the Fathers. St. John Chrysostom writes:

"Do you not know that the priest is the angel of God, he never speaks merely in his own name? To disregard him means disregarding God Himself who appointed him." *Homily 2 on the Second Epistle to Timothy,* No. 2; P.G. Vol. 62 C. 610.

In another place he develops this same thought in greater detail when he writes:

"It is the work of the priest to beget new children unto God in baptism. It is by the hand of the priest that we are clothed with Christ, that we are buried with him and become members of his mystical body, of that body of which he is the Head." *On the Priesthood,* Bk. 3; P.G. Vol. 48. C. 643.

All this power which belongs to the priest as another

Christ is rooted in his unique ability to perform certain actions which are the works of Christ alone:

"When you behold the priest offering the consecrated bread, see in his hand the hand of Christ himself." *Homily 50 on St. Matthew,* P.G. Vol. 58. C. 507.

This view of priestly character and consecration is found in most classical writers, and the differentiation of this power from the general priesthood of the people is seen, for example, in St. Thomas. In his commentary on Chapter IV, verse 11, of the Epistle to the Ephesians, he points out that St. Paul gives the apostles first place in his enumeration of Christ's gifts to the Church. The next place is held by the extension of the apostles and their successors — priests.[19]

The Council speaks of the union of priest with Christ as rooted in his ordination and expressed in the Sacrifice of the Mass.

"Through the ministry of the bishop, God consecrates priests so that they can share by a special title in the priesthood of Christ. Thus, in performing sacred functions they can act as the ministers of him who in the liturgy continually exercises his priestly office on our behalf by the action of his Spirit."[20]

"As ministers of sacred realities, especially in the Sacrifice of the Mass, priests represent the person of Christ in a special way. He gave himself as a victim to make men holy. Hence priests are invited to imitate the realities they deal with. Since they celebrate the mystery of the Lord's death, they should see to it that every part of their being is dead to evil habits and desires."[21]

The priest is differentiated from all the faithful precisely in terms of his identification with Christ's unique work. It is a differentiation that touches him essentially as well as functionally. The document returns to Sacred

Scripture when it touches the matter of differentiation through sacred Orders. Citing St. Paul, it points out the multiple vocations and charisms within the Church, but notes how certain "powers" identified with carrying on the work of Christ were "handed on" to others.[22] There is no doubt in the document that these powers were specific priestly powers that affected the recipient not only in his capacity to function, but in himself. This reaffirmation of the Synod says that the priesthood is defined in terms of its own reality and not solely under its functional aspect. A priest is described, first, as a specific reality, then as a functionary. Because of his ordination, a priest is able to perform specific actions.[23]

Following the lead of St. Paul, the Synod speaks of the priestly work and office as one of many within a united whole. Within the Church there are various offices and functions that exercise their activity. Yet not all are equal. Nor are all interchangeable. This consecrated variety is as necessary for the life of the Church as is the diversity of bodily parts and functions for human physical well being. This diversity in the ways of participating in Christ's priesthood and their interrelation are basic to the structure of the Church.

"This essential structure of the Church . . . according to the tradition of the Church herself was always and remains the norm."[24]

The precise point of differentiation is the priest's ability to perpetuate Christ within the Church in a manner that is not open to the rest of the faithful, who are nonetheless identified in other ways with Christ and his mission.[25] Without minimizing the sacred vocation of baptism, the Synod highlights the specifically hierarchical nature of the Church. This order rests on the reality of the sacrament of Holy Orders and its ability to differentiate within the Christian community. The distinction, fundamental and essential, between the priesthood common to all the faithful and the ministerial office, stated in the words of Vatican Council II, is "one of essence and not only of degree."[26]

By his ordination the priest is defined.

"He is in the midst of the Christian community which lives by the Spirit, even with his personal deficiencies, as a pledge of the salvific presence of Christ."[27]

When speaking in the context of the sacrament of Orders and "essential" difference between the priesthood of the laity and that of an ordained minister, the document is clearly indicating a radical differentiation conferred in Sacred Orders. The priest is not only identified by his ordination but is defined by it. In it he receives a new closeness with Christ that is described by the document as a "configuring" with Christ.

The Synod makes no effort to explain how this configuring takes place. Nor does it offer a clarification of the meaning of "essential difference." But it is abundantly clear that Sacred Orders change a priest and somehow make him what he was not before, and give him powers which he did not have before ordination. In "configuration" with Christ is understood somehow an inauguration into Christ's life and work that alters the person and gives him powers that fundamentally distinguish him from the rest of believers. The identification with Christ is expressed in the unique works assigned the priesthood.

This theological point is developed within the document. The text emphasizes heavily the mediation of Christ's activity through the Church. Even the outline of the document makes clear the intention of the Synod to indicate that it is the Church that is "the way to the person and mystery of Christ."[28] The priest, as commissioned by the Church, is the one united to Christ.

As Christ is the teacher, witness, and means of salvific sacrifice, so is the priest. The font and source of all priestly existence and activity is Christ. The Synod sees identification with Christ as constitutive of priestly life. A priest is not a reflection of what Christ was: he makes locally present the priestly life and work that is Christ's; he is a consecrated man who on the most interior level shares the mission and work of Christ.

"By the laying on of hands there is communicated a gift of the Holy Spirit which cannot be lost (*cf.* 2 Tm 1, 6). This reality configures the ordained minister to Christ, consecrates him and makes him a sharer in Christ's mission under the two-fold aspect of authority and service."[29]

This relationship with Christ is permanent, since the priest is "irrevocably" joined to Christ. His "new life" is expressed in a "character, as it is called in the tradition of the Church," which binds the priest in the Church to Christ. Identification on this level is not confined to extrinsic functions. It is an interior unity with Jesus Christ and constitutes the priestly ministry.

The priest is a priest because of his identification with Christ. The expression of that identity with Christ is found in the works of the priest. Certain powers are his because he is one with Christ, and because he has been chosen and ordained to perform specific works he has been given special powers and an identity with Christ. The union with Christ is expressed in the exercise of that unique power of the priest which permits him to perpetuate the work of Christ. The Synod sees this as "the essential work of the Apostles," a work which the priest performs:

1. by effectively proclaiming the gospel;
2. by gathering together and leading the community;
3. by remitting sin;
4. by celebrating the Eucharist;
5. by exercising Christ's work of redeeming mankind and glorifying God perfectly.

In brief, the priest is a sharer in the function of "sanctifying, teaching, and governing the faithful."[30]

NOTES

1. I, 4.
2. I, 1, 3 and 4.
3. *The Documents of Vatican II,* Walter Abbott, ed., (New York: America Press, 1966), "Priests," by Guilford C. Young, p. 527.
4. IV, 1, 2, 3 and 4. English version, National Catholic News Service Documentation, April 29, 1971.
5. I, 5.
6. "Exegesis non modo multa quidem de Iesu et eisu saeculo nos fecit intelligere, sed nonnullis etiam aditum ad Iesu personam immediatum reddidit difficiliorem.

"Vita autem praesertim sacerdotis in clara ac profunda cum Iesu necessitudine est posita. Illum debet sequi, illum ministerio suo repraesentare, ab illo ergo in tota sua vita referre indolem. Non datur ad Christum validus accessus nisi in promptu quis sit, objectionibus quibusvis neglectis, ad eius sequelam."

Relatio: "Circuli minoris linguae Germanicae" (in sessione Synodi plenaria die 8vo), p. 3. (Unpublished report of the German language section). This language group limited itself to the study and amplification of the propositions of the International Theological Commission as related to the needs of the Synod's text.

All references to interventions and/or reports either in the hall of the Synod meeting or in the study groups will be by the name of the speaker and/or group represented and the date of the intervention. The note "unpublished" indicates that the source material is still in the process of preparation for publication and is found in the Vatican Synod Office.

7. Et Acta Apostolorum (Act 20: 28) et epistola prima S. Petri (1 Petr 5: 2 seq.) id pastoris officium secundum Christi Spiritum in Ecclesiis exercendum esse testantur. Petro expresse Jesus ut gregem suam pascat mandavit et simul cum suae crucis fore participem promisit (Io 21: 17–19). Quod mandatum explendum significat specificum muneris sacerdotalis. Oblationem ipsius Christi praesentem reddit normativa Evangelii praedicatione, fraterno in Ecclesia ministerio, collectione et regimine communitatis ecclesiasticae, remissione peccatorum, summo autem modo Eucharistiae celebratione, cui praesidet vi potestatis sacerdotalis sacrae ordinatione receptae solium sacerdotis est. Unde sacerdos etiam Ecclesiae unitatem repraesentat et ab ea stat mandatus oratione sua et vita sua coram Deo." Relatio: Circuli minoris linguae Germaniae (unpublished), p. 4.

8. The Synod was broken down into the following language groups: Latin, English, French, Spanish, Portuguese and German. Their function was to discuss in detail the text and interventions made by the speakers. They then presented a summary of their conclusions to the sub-commission responsible for the drawing up of the final version of the text. In all the language group reports it is noted that the document sought to stress the priesthood from the point of view of Christ's mission and activity and the priest's share therein.

9. "Le sacerdoce ministeriel est, dans l'Eglise, une participation au sacredoce eternal du Christ, permettant a des hommes choisis de Dieu, de rendre réelement present, 'en tout temps et en tout lieu' . . . Homme-Dieu." Intervention of Archbishop Augustin Farah, Melchite Archbishop of Tripoli, October 2, 1971, p. 1 (unpublished text: "Le sacerdoce ministeriel à la lumière de la Tradition Orientale").

10. *Ibid.*, p. 2.

11. The English edition of the document is entitled: Declaration in defense of the Catholic doctrine on the Church against certain errors of the present day (Vatican City: Typis Polyglottis Vaticanis, 1973), p. 17 and note 56.

12. I, 4.

13. *Ibid.*

14. *Ibid.*

15. I, 5.

16. The *Dogmatic Constitution on the Church,* No. 10.

17. St. Thomas Aquinas, *Summa Theologica,* Part II, Q. 82, Art. 1 (New York: Benziger Brothers, 1947), pp. 2504-5.

18. Karl Rahner, *Theological Dictionary* (New York: Herder and Herder, 1965), p. 71. For the defined teaching of the Church see the Council of Trent, Session VII, Decree on the Sacraments, Canon 9 (D. 1609).

19. *Commentaria in Omnes S. Pauli Apostoli Epistolas* (Turin: Ed. Marietti, 1929), II, 49.

20. *Ministry and Life of Priests,* No. 5.

21. *Ibid.,* No. 23.

22. The text cites 2 Cor 5: 18ff. to establish that St. Paul was "conscious of acting by Christ's mission and mandate." Then in 2 Tm 1:6 and Ti 1:5 it sees this mandate being passed on with the obligation that it be continued by a handing "on to yet others" (I, 4).

23. I, 4 documents the scriptural basis for the assertion that differentiation according to specific powers within the Church is from apostolic times.

"Among the various charisms and services, the priestly ministry of the New Testament, which continues Christ's function as mediator, and which in essence and not merely in degree is distinct from the common priesthood of all the faithful (*cf.* LG 10), alone perpetuates the essential work of the apostles."

24. *Ibid.*

25. *Ibid.*: See The *Dogmatic Constitution on the Church,* No. 10: "Though they differ from one another in essence and not only in degree, the common priesthood of the faithful and the ministerial or hierarchical priesthood are nonetheless interrelated. Each of them in its own special way is a participation in the one priesthood of Christ."

26. *Ibid.*

27. I, 5.

28. I, 2.

29. I, 5.

30. I, 4.

5. The Priest as Witness

EVERY TIME THE Synod names one of the works of a priest, we find that it is an act of Christ's unique spiritual healing and redeeming power. The first of these deeds of the priest is the proclamation of the gospel. This call to proclamation is the foundation stone for the work of witnessing to the message of Christ. In accepting this task and carrying out its obligation in the realm of verbal testimony, the priest participates in the mission of Christ as the Truth, the Light of the world. In so doing he brings faith to men who depend solely on faith to reach

God. The priest as herald of the salvation of Christ becomes an official spokesman for Christ and the gospel. In this capacity the witness is bound to hand on intact the good news as he received it. He is a witness to the truth. In the words of the Synod, the priest as witness is the "guarantor" of the gospel.

"He is the guarantor both of the first proclamation of the gospel for the gathering together of the Church and of the ceaseless renewal of the Church . . ."[1]

The patristic tradition on witness is strong. St. Cyprian writes on the point that priests are to witness to Christ in their words and deeds that others may come to see and know Christ:

"For if we are priests of God and Christ I can find no better model for us to follow than God and Christ, especially since our Lord says in the gospel: 'I am the light of the world. He who follows me does not walk in darkness, but will have the light in me!' " *Epistula,* 63, P.L. Vol. 4. C. 385.

St. John Chrysostom writing on the particular place of witness in the life of a priest notes:

"Even though his [the priest's] life may be altogether blameless, he will be plunged into hell along with sinners if he has not taken a zealous interest in preaching to you and in all those who have been entrusted to him." *Homily 86 on St. John,* P.G. Vol. 59. C. 471.

In one sense, the priestly function of witness can be seen as given special emphasis by the Synod to the point of being called its major consideration on the priesthood today. The document begins by recalling Christ's role as eternal witness to the Father. The same opening paragraph speaks of the mission of Christ to witness the truth.

"Jesus Christ . . . whom the Father sanctified and sent into the world proclaimed to the world the good news . . ."[2]

The document then draws a parallel between the work of Christ as a witness and that of the apostles and the Church. Next, the document — at great length in comparison to the rest of the text — outlines the early Church's approach to the mission of witness. Even in its application to secular matters of the priest's power, the Synod speaks of the witness mission of the priest.

"The proper mission entrusted by Christ to the priest as to the Church is not of the political, economic or social order, but of the religious order."[3]

This particular sentence is quite clear. Its echo is found in the patristic tradition of the Church. St. John Chrysostom writes of the nature of a priest's work in devoting himself exclusively to the eternal salvation of others: *Homily 86 on St. John,* P.G. Vol. 59. C. 471. St. Gregory the Great writes of the danger that occurs when a priest devotes his time and energies to works other than the care of the faithful and the works of the Church. He speaks directly on the political engagement of priests, and notes that this leaves "his flock without a shepherd" and places the faithful in a position where they "cannot see the light of truth because the mind of their pastor is intent on earthly cares . . ." *Regulae Pastoralis Liber,* pars. 2, P.L. Vol. 77. C. 39.

The function of the witness is indispensable in relation to the faith. There can be no diffusion of the knowledge of the kingdom among men unless those called to live in the kingdom tell others of it. Since no one can see the kingdom or supernatural realities that ground it, they have to be told of them. Grace, life eternal, redemption are not to be known unless one hears of them. They cannot be discovered as they were revealed unless those who have received the "good news" of them are willing to tell others of them.

The priest must, then, testify not only to the Person of Jesus but to the content of his faith. As a witness to the content of the faith, his principal characteristics are two: to carry the words of life to those who are to believe and have no other way of coming to them, and to testify to those words and acts as they were given.

"Each priest shares in the special responsibility of preaching the whole of the Word of God and of interpreting it according to the faith of the Church."[4]

In this aspect of his priesthood, the priest reflects the work and action of Christ. Jesus speaking of his role as the incarnate witness of the Father notes that he does nothing on his own authority but only what he has been taught by the Father. The witness absorbs the message, the truth, but always remains subject to it and obedient before it. The message is not his to change, alter, or distort. The witness is to pass on the knowledge — and, therefore, the life — through this testimony. Christ, in the Incarnation — by assuming our nature — adopted a method by which the presence of God could be made known to man. Each witness to Christ participates in that mission and in its limitations. The mission remains the same: to testify to the truth of God as revealed, that through that truth all may live. The witness to the truth as received must be carried on in the world as that world is, through human signs and words, by human means.

The witness of the revelation of Christ will stand in relation to the faith as it is received, as Christ stood in relation to the mystery of his father in its revelation to him.

> "He is the image of the Father and manifestation of the unseen God. By emptying himself and by being raised up he brought us into the fellowship of the Holy Spirit, which he lives with the Father."[5]

The document places the witness mission of the priest on the level of a share in Christ's mission and at the same time notes the limitations that each witness will face as Christ faced them in his own Incarnation.

To testify to the faith is to participate in the revealing action of the Incarnate Christ who spoke for the Father, that the Father's life might belong to others. The priest shares in that mystery of spreading the knowledge of God by the act of testifying to what is the faith. But that witness must participate in the limitation that is incarnation. The Son of God could use human words, signs and institutions to reach men with his news of the Father and life in his presence. Human words, signs and structures must continue the work of Christ's Revelation. The limitations of individual witness become apparent. Each believer who is prepared to testify to Christ's kingdom among men must do so in words and signs that are understood among men. He cannot claim to have or impart a directly received understanding of the kingdom. His faith also is a received one. Therefore, his testimony must reflect the testimony as given by the entire community of believers. This extends even to the wording of that tradition or "handing on of the good news" when the wording is that specifically confirmed by the entire community. In this manner does each individual witness give his testimony in the larger context of the living witness of the Church. The articulation of the testimony of the entire Church as seen in the creeds is the property of the entire Church. Each believer must testify to the truth in relationship to that witness borne by the whole community of believers. Individual witness participates in the ministry of the unique witness, Christ, but only as a minister of the truth in union with the believing Church.

In this united action, the document seems a fulfillment of both the "personal and social aspects of the announcement of the gospel." By a united witness, the Church not only preaches conversion to God to individual men, but also, to the best of her ability, "as the conscience of humanity, she addresses society itself."[6]

To witness is to proclaim before another the truth of a specific reality. One aspect of witness is that it is related to the truth as a body of beliefs. Witness in this sense means to make known to others the faith. Christ, the Eternal Word of the Father, is, of course, the only direct witness to the Father. All other witnesses must somehow share in the one eternal testimony offered by Christ. "I know where I came from and where I am going" (Jn 8:14). The son "does only what he sees the Father doing: what the Father does the Son does. For the Father loves the Son and shows him all his works. I do nothing on my own authority, but in all that I say, I have been taught by my Father" (Jn 8:29). The Son, as the one who has to dispense life to all men, does so as the living witness to the Father. His witness is the light and that light as the knowledge or revelation of the Father is life. Therefore, to accept Christ is at both one and the same to know him and live a fuller life in Him. But all this depends upon the successful work of some witness.[7]

The document ties in this line of thought with the Council Decree on the Ministry and Life of Priests, which it quoted in explaining how the role of witness is a one. "Priests participate in the office of the apostles . . . They shoulder the sacred task of the gospel . . . Their ministry takes its start from the gospel message . . . They cannot be ministers of Christ unless they are witnesses and dispensers of a life other than this earthly one."[8] Both the Council and the Synod tie together the witness aspect of the priestly mission and his office as minister of the sacramental life. In this way the aspect of the priest's life as witness to the mysteries of God is greatly emphasized.[9]

NOTES

1. I, 4.
2. I, 1.
3. I, 7.
4. II, I, 1.
5. I, 1.
6. II, I, 1.
7. II, I, 2.
8. *Ministry and Life of Priests,* No. 3.
9. II, I, 1.

6. *The Priesthood: Sacramental Witness*

TRADITIONALLY, THE PRIEST has been called the dispenser of the mysteries of God. And certainly, within the context of his work as witness, the priest is the source of grace through the great mystery which is the Eucharist.

Whatever else the priest is, he is the source of sacramental contact with Christ. The framework within which the Christian reaches God is a sacramental one. It is the priest who "makes Christ the Saviour . . . sacramentally present . . ."[1] The Synod lists two sacraments particularly dependent upon the priest. In his function of "remitting sin and celebrating the Eucharist," the priest brings the redeeming Christ into the lives of the faithful.

In both these two instances the priest acts uniquely in the person of Christ. He functions as Christ in "remitting sin and presiding over and effecting the sacrificial banquet."[2] In doing so the priest also builds the community. For by bringing human life into contact with the divine life, the priest performs the first essential function that leads to the establishment of God's kingdom among men.

There is no ambiguity either in the teaching tradition of the Church or in its documents, especially those of Vatican Council II, about the fact that the Eucharistic Sacrifice remains the most important, the crowning action in the life of a priest. In the Mass the priest is acting not only in the name of but in the person of Christ to re-present the sacrifice Jesus made at Calvary. All priestly functions take their beginning and end in this sacred sacramental action just as the whole meaning and purpose of all Christ's activities are summed up and explicable only in terms of the Cross. All the priest's duties, actions and witness-functions must be rooted in the Eucharist. All priestly witness must revolve around the Mass just as do all the sacraments around the Eucharist. The Council at great length made this clear.[3]

"By baptism men are brought into the People of God. By the sacrament of penance sinners are reconciled to God and the Church. By the oil of the sick the ailing find relief. And, especially by the celebration of Mass, men offer sacramentally the sacrifice of Christ. In administering all the sacraments, as St. Ignatius Martyr already bore witness in the days of the primitive Church, priests by various titles are bound together hierarchically with the bishop. Thus in a certain way they make him present in every gathering of the faithful.

"The other sacraments, as well as every ministry of the Church and every work of the apostolate, are linked with the holy Eucharist and are directed toward it. For the most blessed Eucharist contains the Church's entire spiritual wealth, that is, Christ himself, our passover and living bread. Through his very flesh, made vital and vitalizing by the Holy Spirit, he offers life to men. They are thereby invited and led to offer themselves, their labors, and all created things together with him.

"Hence the Eucharist shows itself to be the source and the apex of the whole work of preaching the gospel. Those under instruction are introduced by stages to a sharing in the Eucharist. The faithful, already marked with the sacred seal of baptism and confirmation, are through the reception of the Eucharist fully joined to the body of Christ.

"Thus the Eucharistic action is the very heartbeat of the congregation of the faithful over which the priest presides. So priests must instruct them to offer to God the Father the divine Victim in the sacrifice of the Mass and to join to it the offering of their own lives. In the spirit of Christ the Shepherd, priests should train them to submit their sins with a contrite heart to the Church in the sacrament of penance. Thus, mindful of the Lord's words: 'Repent, for the Kingdom of God is at hand' (Mt 4:17), the people will be drawn ever closer to him each day."[3]

The contribution of the Synod to this matter is its reminder that even the Mass, the center of priestly function, is a part of the overall witness of the priest — just as Calvary, though the apex of Christ's redeeming action, was part of His overall saving mission. No priest can claim his witness to be complete if his priestly ministration consists only in saying Mass, any more than can a priest claim to be faithfully extending Christ's Kingdom and work without the Mass. The Synod sees the priestly mission of witness to the world of all Christ came and did as the stuff of the priesthood. The Mass is the apex and summit of priestly action, mission and witness.

"The priestly ministry reaches its summit in the celebration of the Eucharist, which is the source and center of the Church's unity. Only a priest is able to act in the person of Christ in presiding over and effecting the sacrificial banquet wherein the People of God are associated with Christ's offering (*cf.* LG 28)."[4]

By connecting his sacramental powers with his community-building mission, the Synod places an emphasis on the priest's particular quality as the bearer of divine life which makes human community possible. The document follows up what it had to say on the priest as Eucharistic minister by pointing to his role in "building up of the Christian community" (1, 5) and his work in the wider area of "the secular order" (I, 7). The intention seems to be to stress the sacramental function of the priest as leading to the establishment of real Christian community among believers, and also — through its influence and example — the wider area of those who are not believers.

In this work of converting human life to divine life we see another aspect of the Synod's view of the profound nature of the priesthood. Not only is the priest in some way united to Christ, "configured"[5] with him in a unique manner, but he is also able to act as Christ at least in two important areas. He can perform the truly divine act of "remitting" sin and the equally God-like service of effecting the Eucharist. In both cases the document sees this activity as a result of his union with Christ and a means of bringing others to Christ. The first point we see in the priestly state or office that results from ordination. The latter point we must now see in the context of the full priestly mission.

The Synod does not see the priest's identification with Christ as limited to the office of dispensing the sacraments. Rather it sees these as the "summit" of the priestly ministry. In the document even the context of the administration of the sacraments remains the priestly mission of complete witness to Christ. The rest of the mission connected with that office is described as the representation of Christ to the world and the completion of his work in the world. This basically is the priestly ministry of witness or evangelization and that of leading the Christian community or building Christian unity.

"The sacraments are celebrated in conjunction with the proclamationtion of the Word of God and thus develop faith by strengthening it with grace. They cannot be considered of slight importance."[6]

The two tasks — witnessing the word to the world and strengthening the sacramental life of the faithful — work as part of one integrated ministry. The priest witnesses Christ and makes Christ's work present. Therefore, all Christ's works must be part of the priest's ministry. The Synod seems to see each priestly action as a part of his priestly mission. And the overriding norm is the mission of witness given by Christ. The Synod notes the congruity of the witness and sacramental aspects of priestly ministry. In fact, it calls for a unity between them.

The Synod sees that the priest must be endowed with authority, in order to accomplish both personally and socially this unity of sacrament and witness. It sees both evangelization and sacramental life as "demanding" a diaconia of authority.[7] If he is to carry on the ministry of teaching and that of sanctifying, he must also possess spiritual authority. He then works simultaneously on three levels: that of carrying the word that gives faith; that of nourishing the faith by the sacraments; and that of leading the community, formed in faith and the sacraments, with spiritual authority.

Closely following the priestly office of witness is that

of "gathering together and leading the community."[8] This follows on the office of witness. For the priest's living witness is indispensable to the building of the community of the faithful. There can be no diffusion of the knowledge of the Kingdom of God without witnesses to its coming. And as those responsible for the building of the Kingdom assist its growth, they must coordinate and direct its activity. In leading the faithful in matters spiritual, moral, and cultic, the priest functions as Christ in gathering together and leading the community.

Precisely as leader in the Church the priest demonstrates his functional union with Christ the prophet as well as Christ the king. The purely spiritual realm of the priest's leadership is noted when the Synod speaks of the secular or temporal matters that are part of the life of a priest. The priest's involvement in the affairs of human life called secular are limited by the self-imposed concentration on the divine aspect of our existence.

"All truly Christian undertakings are related to the salvation of mankind, which, while it is of an eschatological nature, also embraces temporal matters. Every reality of this world must be subjected to the lordship of Christ. This, however, does not mean that the Church claims technical competence in the secular order, with disregard for the latter's autonomy.

"The proper mission entrusted by Christ to the priest, as to the Church, is not of the political, economic, or social order, but of the religious order (cf. GS 42); yet, in the pursuit of his ministry, the priest can contribute greatly to the establishment of a more just secular order, especially in places where the human problems of injustice and oppression are more serious. He must always, preserve ecclesial communion and reject violence in words or deeds as not being in accordance with the gospel.

"In fact, the word of the gospel which he proclaims in the name of Christ and the Church, and the effective grace of sacramental life which he administers, should free man from his personal and social egoism and foster among men conditions of justice, which would be a sign of the love of Christ present among us (*cf.* GS 58)."[9]

The document apparently bases its conclusion on the separation of temporal or secular affairs from priestly action, upon the supposition stated throughout the document that priests are "witnesses and stewards of another life" (*cf.* PO 3).[10] The first concern of this "steward" is the spiritual welfare of his people. The Synod continues that the priest as witness and spiritual leader must always be aware of his specific qualification as representative of another order than this earthly one. "In order that he may remain a valid sign of unity and be able to preach the gospel in its entirety, the priest can sometimes be obliged to abstain from the exercise of his own rights."[11] And in carrying out his spiritual mission, the priest must center his work in the dual tasks of evangelization and sacramental ministration. For it is in these two aspects of the one mission that the work of building the Kingdom is completed.

"Unity between evangelization and sacramental life is always proper to the ministerial priesthood and must carefully be kept in mind by every priest . . .

"Since the sacraments are truly sacraments of faith (*cf.* SC 59), they require conscious and free participation by every Christian who has the use of reason. This makes clear the great importance of preparation and of a disposition of faith on the part of the person who receives the sacraments; it also makes clear the necessity for a witness of faith on the part of the minister in his entire life and especially in the way he values and celebrates the sacraments themselves."[12]

As a community builder, the priest shares in one of the principal aspects of the mission of the bishop. For as a spiritual leader in the Church, the bishop and therefore the priest must carry on the mission of enlarging Christ's Kingdom on earth and governing it.

But in the light of everything the document says on the spiritual nature of the Kingdom, the service dimension of authority and the faith aspect of the Christian community, it is clear that the community building mentioned by the Synod is the spiritual work of conversion, of life according to gospel dictates, and of union with God. The Kingdom of God is not to be a political unity or a cultural grouping. And so the builders of this community must be aware of its unique character, which stems from the mission given the Church by Christ, the object of the Church, and the means it has to attain its end. This does not mean that the Church will not be visible and structured: all that the document says on structure clearly shows a Church established in a definite visible manner. But the reason for the Church's existence as a visible structure is to help men better form that spiritual community which is the Kingdom of God as it is found in time and space.

The means the Church has to reach her goal are all spiritual means, e.g., the sacraments, prayers, grace. The object is eventually to bring all men to Christ and through him to the Father. Christian community then is a spiritual community that can exist in spite of political or ethnic divisions. Its focus is in another order.

Several points follow from this assertion. The principal work of the community builder will be spiritual. The priest, as the community builder, should see his objective as involving primarily the faith and charity life of those committed to him. This should have consequences in the secular lives of the faithful and should strengthen the unity of the civil, political, and economic community. But the priest's unique contribution is not directly ordered to such ends. His specific area of concentration is that of building a faith community strong enough to live the love of Christ so that the whole community is permeated with the Spirit of Christ. His direct efforts in temporal, secular, and political areas remain secondary to his mission as community builder.

This bring us to the question of the political involvement of priests, particularly in partisan elections where they become the representatives of specific parties and political platforms.

The priest's witness will always touch the political, social, cultural, and economic orders. This is true because his message must touch men where they are. But the question is, "How does he make his witness felt?" Few would say that the priest is to exercise *no* influence in the world of politics. After all, he is part of the larger community and a spokesman for some of its most cherished principles. In his preaching and otherwise, he will necessarily make clear the moral imperatives that are part of the gospel message. This means that at times the priest may find himself holding some positions that are also reflected in the public statements of certain politicians or in the platform of some political party. Such coincidence cannot be avoided. In fact, one would hope that moral judgments expressing Christian values will often be found in the programs and statements of partisan politicians. But when they are not there, the question remains, "How do we see to it that politics and Christian imperatives are mingled?"

One alternative is to have the priest leave aside his ministerial duties and his teaching and preaching office and take to the campaign trail. Another approach is to have the priest in his preaching, exhorting, teaching and example attempt to draw out of those in public office and out of the voters a response worthy of the Gospels.

To many, the credibility of a moral imperative that is too closely linked to a political advantage will seem open to question. It is at this juncture of political expediency with moral principle that one can sometimes find himself open to the charge of tailoring the gospel for the sake of re-election. And it is at this point that the essential incongruity of the priest-partisan office-seeker is found. As priest he is responsible to the gospel. He is obliged to preach its imperatives. But as candidate or office-holder, his loyalties are divided among voters, party bosses, and political expediencies.

There seems to be a parallel here with the idea of a priest in military action. A chaplain is distinguished from a combatant. This is so on account of his specific mission. The military chaplain who serves the pastoral needs of soldiers is by his ordination presumed to be a man for peace. He bears no arms. He leads no charge. He kills no enemies. But he is, nonetheless, in the midst of the fighting. He is there to minister to his people. His service is on another level. His own conviction might very well be that this specific war is justified. He might lament the imperfect state of man that permits the enemy a view different from his own. But he must not take up arms. His service is on another plane. In fact, if called upon as a priest, he ought to be prepared to minister to the enemy.

The priest is to teach, plead, influence, and exhort his fellow-Christians. In his healing ministry he is to be a witness to the ultimate unity of all men and to the law of love that must eventually embrace all peoples. This may involve opposition to some government statements or programs. But what kind of opposition? Should laws be drawn up by priests, or by negotiations between priest-politicians and party bosses? Or should the priest's opposition rather be the influence of conviction? Should it be the Christian faith's power to move men — even in public life — to follow Christ's way?

Again, almost paradoxically, the arrival on the political scene of the priest office-seeker comes at a time when the emphasis within the Church is on the need to free priests from unnecessary duties in the secular order, thus enabling them to concentrate full time and full self on those things which only a priest can do. At the moment, the direction seems to be that of pointing out the need of lay people to help in the administration of Church affairs, in religious institutions and even, with the revival of the permanent diaconate and permission to distribute communion, in sacramental matters. But all this has been done under the banner of the freeing of priests to concentrate on those things which only they can do. Within the Church from the days of Paul's Letters, there have always been recognized areas of different competency. The most obvious one, of course, is that connected with sacred Orders. But others are almost equally obvious. The whole tendency since Vatican Council II seems to be towards a reinforcement of the distinctive role and work within the Church and the secular community that are the laity's. The document on priestly life and formation speaks of the priest's need to address himself to the spiritual needs of God's people both in example and in ministry. But in the *Pastoral Constitution on the Church,* the area of politics is commended with special care and concern to the laymen who are suited for it. The Synod recalls and confirms this very explicitly. The same Synod rejects the idea of priests in partisan politics so clearly and strongly that the matter seems closed.

According to the Council, Christian men and women have a major, active part to play in making this world a real community of justice and love. Specific talents and particular callings have long been considered part of God's plan to build such a better world. This does not mean to say that the priest is excluded from such a project. It merely means that his work is on a different plane. He is to keep alive the ideal of Christian unity. He is to spread the Faith. He has the task of carrying the healing power of the sacraments to a world sick and torn. At the altar his mediation is to be active and fruitful.

As a minister of the Kingdom of God, the priest must form God's Kingdom in the people entrusted to him. In doing this he builds the spiritual realm that is God's world. This type of community building requires a specific viewpoint. It rests on faith and has a strong eschatological aspect. There are certain suppositions that are part of the world view within which the Christian and the priest see the work of "community building."

For the Christian, man has come into conflict with his Creator. Man's egotism, his ability to sin and the actual fact of his rejection of God have led to a world filled with injustice. Yet, in the midst of all that confusion of goals and rejection of values that make up the modern world, there remains in the Christian vision an answer. That answer is Jesus. Christ came to reconcile once and for all man with God and men with men. His mission was one of challenge. He offered men a new world — a new style of life.

Such a Christian view is the result of revelation. We only know of Jesus' new world through Jesus' revelation. It rests on the conviction that the God of creation has given life to all men and therefore is equally their Father.

It accepts the redemption of Christ as the means to brotherhood among all men. And it looks to the Spirit of God as the bond that unites all men in peace and reconciliation. This is what the Synod means by the spiritual powers of the priest as a builder of Christian community.

Original sin, personal guilt, redemption, grace and the hope of final reconciliation with God are the supernatural realities that make up the world of the believer. For him they are the facts against which the struggle to build a Christian community of justice in our day should be seen. These facts become the stuff of a Christian world order. With this view the believer proceeds as if the only real and lasting reconciliation will be that which rests upon God's plan as he has revealed it.

The community to be built by the believer has specific qualities. The priest first recognizes these distinctive aspects of the Kingdom, as applied to man's day-to-day life, and then he tries to teach them. Not every detail of community life, however, is the result of revelation.

Priests are in the words of the Synod to be the builders of the community of God on earth by being the witnesses and stewards of another life. By their action and lives priests are to be the heralds of the faith in the life to come.

"Priests, without being of the world and without taking it as their model, must nevertheless live in the world (*cf.* PO 3, 17; Jn 17: 14–16), as witnesses and stewards of another life (*cf.* PO 3)."[13]

In addition, then, to his role as witness to the word of God, the priest is also a community builder. This function as his witness is the result of his participation in the call and mission of the bishop. He, as a priest, shares in the whole spectrum of work that is the mission of the bishop.

To build a Christian community is one of the functions of the priest because it was one of the priestly works of Christ and was passed on to his Church as a continuing obligation. The nature of the community that he is building will determine in no small part the way in which the priest goes about building his community. And since the Kingdom of God is a spiritual one, the priest will need to use those spiritual means left by Christ for his Church. The activity will be directed to the spiritual formation of his fellow-Christians so that in their activity and response they too will reflect the community of faith and love that is the Church. In this work the priest has a principal role and carries out his work as community builder.

NOTES

1. I, 4.
2. *Ibid.*
3. *Ministry and Life of Priests,* No. 5.
4. I, 4.
5. I, 5.
6. II, I, 1.
7. *Ibid.*
8. I, 4.
9. I, 7.
10. II, I, 2.
11. *Ibid.*
12. II, I, 1.
13. II, I, 2.

7. *Leadership*

"AUTHORITY" IS NOT a fashionable word today. But it refers to something that still has a place within the Church, as it has within any society, human or divine. Authority within the Church, however, is essentially an authority of service, and it exists to gather together and lead the Christian community in the way of the Lord.

Since the priest is to function as Christ "by gathering together and leading the community," he exercises also a share in the authority of Christ the "head of the Church." The principal object of this authority is work towards a unity of the whole Church.[1]

"His ministry always tends towards the unity of the whole Church and to the gathering together in her of all men. Each individual community of faithful needs fellowship with the bishop and the universal Church. In this way the priestly ministry too is essentially communitarian within the presbyterium and with the bishop who, preserving communion with the successor of Peter, is a part of the body of bishops. This holds also for priests who are not in the immediate service of any community or who work in remote and isolated territories. Religious priests, also, within the context of the special purpose and structure of their institute, are indissolubly part of a mission which is ecclesially ordered."[2]

What authority the priest has in building community rests on the share he has in Christ's mission to make of this world a kingdom of believers. The works of such a community builder must therefore be essentially directed to the order of faith and the establishment of Christ's salvation among men. Such a community will be a manifestation of Christ's glory while the priest's authority in building that kingdom will be a manifestation of the "power" of the Lord.

The Church is the context of this priestly authority and the needs of its well being determine the exercise of that authority. The community of priests and their union with the bishop forms the framework for the exercise of priestly authority which at all times must work in harmony with the Church's purpose and effect the spiritual good of men and the unity of them in the Church.

That authority does not belong to the minister as his own: it is a manifestation of the *"Exousia"* (i.e., the power) of the Lord, by which the priest is an ambassador of Christ in the eschatological work of reconciliation (*cf.* 2 Cor 5:18–20). He also assists the conversion of human freedom to God for the building up of the Christian community.[3]

The Council in the Decree on the Ministry and Life of

Priests notes that priestly power is a result of priestly consecration.

"To the acquisition of this perfection (demanded by Christ) priests are bound by a special claim, since they have been consecrated to God in a new way by the reception of orders. They have become living instruments of Christ the eternal priest, so that through the ages they can accomplish His wonderful work of reuniting the whole society of men with heavenly power." (No. 12)

Priestly authority, then, comes from Christ through the Church. Its purpose is that of all authority — to build up the community and help its members work well together. In the Church this authority is traditionally pictured, from the days of Christ, as a shepherd leading his flock with loving care. The end of the journey for the flock is the Kingdom of God. The purpose of the authority of the shepherd is to lead to that Kingdom.

"They (priests) should act toward men, not as seeking to win favor but in accord with the demands of Christian doctrine and life. They should teach and admonish men as dearly beloved sons, according to the words of the Apostle: 'Be urgent in season, out of season; reprove, entreat, rebuke with all patience and teaching' (2 Tim. 4,2)" (No. 6)

Leadership, in this sense, is directed to the education of the faithful in those mysteries that comprise the faith of the believer and give ground to his charity.

"As educators in the faith, priests must see to it, either by themselves or through others, that the faithful are led individually in he Holy Spirit to a development of their own vocation as required by the gospel, to a sincere and active charity, and to that freedom with which Christ has made us free." (No. 6)

All this teaching authority and leadership commission

within the Church is directly, says the Synod, to the building up of the unity of the Church. Priests in the exercise of their office must reconcil "all men in the love of Christ" and pay "attention to the dangers of divisions."[4] Authority does not exist to divide the Church and change her teaching. "The Church must nevertheless always proclaim to the world the Gospel in its entirety. Each priest shares in the special responsibility of preaching the whole of the Word of God and of interpreting it according to the faith of the Church."[5]

This priestly mission requires authority in matters spiritual. For it is in the realm of the spirit that the great and decisive battle for the hearts of men and women is won or lost. The priest has his authority to help raise up a new creation, a new humanity — born in the Spirit of Christ.

> "The whole priestly mission is dedicated to that new humanity which Christ, the conqueror of death, raises up in the world through the Spirit. This humanity takes its origin 'not of blood, nor of the will of the flesh, nor of the will of man, but of God.' (Jn. I.13)"[6]

The Synod speaks of this mission as giving identity to the priest. "Priests thus find their identity to the extent that they fully live the mission of the Church and exercise it . . . as pastors and ministers of the Lord in the Spirit, in order to fulfil by their work the plan of salvation in history."[7]

The exercise of the diaconia of authority as it is explained in these documents falls into two categories: (1) teaching truth with authority, and (2) directing the community in the path of unity. The first point is centered in the need and right of the priest to communicate with authority the word of God and teaching of the

Gospels. Here the service is one of authoritatively interpreting the word of God for his day and his flock. The second point is centered in the priest's mission to maintain and build Christian community with the authority of Christ's wish that they all be one. Relative to the first point we have seen the priest's obligation to witness the word of God, and the necessary authority to do so that he derives from the principal witness, the bishop. We have also seen the limits placed on this authority by its nature of a service within the Church, offered to God's people but subject to the integrity and continuity that each minister of the word must give his message.

The authority to build community is in a like manner a service that is limited by the nature of the community of faith that the priest undertakes to confirm and build. On this particular point the Synod notes the specifically spiritual nature of Christ's Kingdom.

> "The proper mission entrusted by Christ to the priest, as to the Church, is not of the political, economic, or social order, but of the religious order (*cf.* GS 42); yet, in the pursuit of his ministry, the priest can contribute greatly to the establishment of a more just secular order, especially in places where the human problems of injustice and oppression are more serious. He must always, however, preserve ecclesial communion and reject violence in words or deeds as not being in accordance with the gospel."[8]

The Synod notes that the test of unity remains "communion with the successor of Peter."[9] Following its logic, the Synod sees the priestly office exercising its role of leadership within the Church according to the normative leadership of the successor of Peter expressed in the local bishop. Both functions of the service of authority remain directed by the overriding bond of communion with Peter. Doctrinal unity will find expression in the identity between the message proclaimed by any priestly minister throughout the world and that proclaimed by the teaching office of the pope. The spiritual dimensions of the Kingdom will also be defined in relation to the guidance of the Holy Father in those matters that relate to the building of the Kingdom.

The need to maintain a unity between evangelization and the sacramental life is one of the reasons given for the exercise of a "diaconia" of authority within the Church. There cannot be a well-ordered community of faithful united in faith and charity without some direction and leadership. The leadership element is founded both in the natural need of any society to direct its affairs and in the God-given structure of the Kingdom. The unique element of the Church's authority element is its basic attitude of service. The exercise of the diaconia of authority is governed by the intrinsic reality that this diaconia is one of a service in unity and presidency of charity. The priest must be conscious then that he leads the community in bringing it into unity in faith as he builds it up in charity; and he must be conscious that these two aspects of the ministry cannot be separated. His fidelity to the word of God in preaching the Gospels according to the Church's tradition must exist alongside his dedication to the building of God's Kingdom.

"An enduring evangelization and well-ordered sacramental life of the community demand, by their nature, a diaconia of authority, that is, a serving of unity and a presiding over charity. Thus the mutual relationship between evangelization and the celebration of the sacraments is clearly seen in the mission of the Church. A separation between the two would divide the heart of the Church to the point of imperiling the faith, and the priest, who is dedicated to the service of unity in the community, would be gravely distorting his ministry."[10]

Both aspects of the Gospel message become the duty of the priest's ministration. The personal and social sides of the Kingdom of God become part of the preaching of the witness.

"Impelled by the need to keep in view both the personal and social aspects of the announcement of the gospel, so that in it an answer may be given to all the more fundamental questions of men (*cf.* CD 13), the Church not only preaches conversion to God to individual men, but also, to the best of her ability, as the conscience of humanity, she addresses society itself and performs a prophetic function in society's regard, always taking pains to effect her own renewal."[11]

Within the Synod's view of the Church as the witness to Christ's final victory, two aspects of the priestly ministry stand out. First of all, the priest is one called to provide the believer with the immediate contacts with Christ that are the sacraments. The ministry of witness by word and deed is tied in with the sacramental ministry in that both announce in different ways the coming of God's final manifestation when the Kingdom will be completed. As a witness and minister of the Kingdom as it is found on earth, the priest enjoys what the Synod calls a "diaconia" of authority. The priest is to function with spiritual authority within and over the community of believers. The scope of his authority is defined by the nature of the Kingdom and the particular needs of the faithful in relation to the priest.

Such a view of the Church leaves room for a real leadership element within the community. But the leaders are determined by their differentiation through orders which permits them to share in a fuller degree the ministry of witness and the sacramental office of the priest.

NOTES

1. II, I, 1.
2. I, 6.
3. I, 5.
4. II, I, 1.
5. *Ibid.*
6. *Ibid.*
7. *Ibid.*
8. I, 7.
9. I, 6.
10. II, I, 1.
11. *Ibid.*

8. *Presbyterium*

In order to round out the Synod's work on the priesthood, it is necessary to touch on one of the theological statements of that meeting's document that is really a practical application of the theology found throughout the text of the document. The presbyterium as it is seen by the Synod is an expression of the active ministry of the priesthood found in a concrete form. In order to complete a study of the Synod's position on the presbyterium, we must refer in no small part to the second half of the document. However, the theological foundations for the theology stated in the second part of the text are to be found in the Doctrinal Part of the text.

The statement in Part II which calls for a Council of

Priests and at the same time sums up the theological premise of the Council is found in II, II, 1: "The Council of Priests, which is of its nature something diocesan, is an institutional manifestation of the brotherhood among priests which has its basis in the sacrament of Orders."

This statement is the result of the more developed theological statements of the priesthood found in Part I, numbers 4 and 5.

The idea of a Council of Priests did not originate with the Synod. Two years earlier, the Vatican office for priests — the Sacred Congregation for the Clergy — published a circular letter on Priest Councils calling for one to be established in each diocese.[1]

The second major part of Part Two of the Synod's document is concerned with the relationships that follow upon ordination. Three principal assertions form the foundation for this section of the document. They are:

1. Priests share in a special way the mission of the bishop because they participate in Holy Orders.
2. All priests are united with each other because they share the same sacramental bond.
3. The body of priests taken together is the presbyterium.

The first point has been discussed above in the section dealing with the mediated nature of priestly Orders. The bishop shares with the priests that mission he has from Christ because priests share with him Sacred Orders.

In the Synod, the primacy in the local Church of the bishop was highlighted. In terms of his teaching, worshiping and ministering primacy, each priest is designated a sharer. The bishop, in this view, is the center of the Church.[2] His actions and words are to spread the word and announce the Kingdom. To do this effectively, he calls others out of the community to be identified more intimately with his work. The priest is then ordained, selected, set apart for others. His designation is part of his new being. It is the source of his mission. The priest is consecrated by the Church, through his selection and distinct calling. In this view, priestly ordination is not seen as the mere selection by the community of a functionary for sanctuary duty. But at the same time the priest's dependent relationship to the bishop who is the "first and principal priest" ties the priest to a functional role within the Church.

Seemingly, the Synod defines priests in terms of their work and their ordination. Both aspects of priestly life are bound up with the call that the priest receives to share the mission of the bishop. In such a view, the work of the Kingdom becomes the job of the priest because he is set apart to share the task originally entrusted to the bishop. The priest is described essentially in terms of what he is, and functionally in terms of what he must do. It is in this latter area that a working relationship with the bishop comes to the fore.

"The service of authority on the one hand and the exercise of not passive obedience on the other should be carried out in a spirit of faith, mutual charity, filial and friendly confidence and constant and patient dialogue. Thus the collaboration and responsible cooperation of priests with the bishop will be sincere, human and at the same time supernatural (*cf.* LG 28; CD 15; PO 7)."[3]

Since the oneness of priests with the bishop rests on the same calling they have received, the identical mission they enjoy and the priesthood they share, the bishop must be considered as part of the presbyterium.

"The Council of Priests, which is of its nature something diocesan, is an institutional manifestation of the brotherhood among priests which has its basis in the sacrament of Orders."[4]

The presbyterium as a single body of priests necessarily includes the person of the bishop, since he has the fullness of the priesthood in the local church. The Synod stresses that within the local church, united with each other, the priests are co-workers with the bishop. If they are structured to give expression in their cooperation, it is as a unit tied intrinsically to the bishop. Those selected to speak for the whole body of priests should be aware of their ministerial dependence upon and cooperation with the head of the local Christian community. For it is the result of his unity with the bishop that the individual priest shares in the mission that belongs to the presbyterium.

Here the Synod is speaking of expressions of the presbyterium in terms of its theological foundation. There is little place, it seems in this view, for a conception of the priests' council as a "congress" or "labor union" "outside of" and "opposed" to the bishop. Rather, the Synod sees priests, united in any organization, as one with the bishop because of the sacred work they have to do together.

"The Priests' Council is an institution in which priests recognize, at a time when variety in the exercise of their ministry increases every day, that they are mutually complementary in serving one and the same mission of the Church."[5]

The presbyterium is not an independent entity. But neither is it merely an empty word. This should be an instrument that gives voice to the thoughts and opinions of the priests who work within a given local church. If all priests are participants in the work of the bishop, then somehow all priests should be effectively represented in any organization that speaks for the entire presbyterium.

The second principal assumption of the document is that each priest by his ordination is united with every other priest.

> "Since priests are bound together by an intimate sacramental brotherhood and by their mission, and since they work and plan together for the same task, some community of life or a certain association of life shall be encouraged among them and can take various forms, including non-institutional ones. This shall be allowed for by the law itself through opportune norms and by renewed or newly-discovered pastoral structures."[6]

The Second Vatican Council's document on the *Bishop's Pastoral Office* expresses the unity of the presbyterium in terms of the single common effort of both bishop and priest in "securing the welfare of souls."[7]

This description is reductively a pragmatic one, since it sees the bond of unity among priests and bishops as one centered in their work. But the same document is quick to point out that it is the sacrament of Orders that makes possible the work in which the priests find their unity.[8] As the apostles were united in their work as fishers of men, so too does the fundamental unity between priests and bishops lie in their call to win all men to the cause of Christ. And with this call comes ordination and an intrinsic relationship to every other priest sharing the sacrament of Orders. Because he is called to the same work and ordained to do that job, each priest is united to all priests. The bond is an intrinsic one following on the sacrament of Orders they share and a pragmatic one following upon the same work in which they participate. As a co-worker with his bishop and fellow-priests, each priest has, besides his priestly character, a functional basis for his oneness with them. He is doing the same work. He is, in the words of the Council, "pasturing a single portion of the Lord's flock."[9]

All this the Council speaks of in its teaching either on the Church or on the priesthood. In the documents the *Bishop's Pastoral Office* and *Ministry and Life of Priests*[10] two essential notes stand out. The priesthood is the extension of the bishop and, therefore, a unit that works in conjunction with him; and it is a body or brotherhood one enters into through ordination and therefore is a sacramental unity and not merely a functional entity. As a person bearing the dignity of Sacred Orders, the priest has a special fundamental tie with each of his brother priests and with his bishop. This gives him a claim to unity with them. The bedrock of the presbyterium is, therefore, the ordained priesthood of Christ shared by all its members. When a man is ordained he enters into a special relationship with Christ. This relationship is personal and intimate, while at the same time public and shared. As a private relationship it is the strength of his spiritual life. His ministry as a vital and life-giving work springs from the face-to-face knowledge of Christ that is his as a priest, one chosen. And, to a great extent, his priesthood will depend on his ability to cultivate this chosen friendship relationship with Christ. As a public and shared calling, the priesthood will have another side to it, a communal aspect. The priest stands before God and God's people as one called publicly to serve the Church in a specific capacity. The Church has always understood the priesthood as a public ministry and not a private and purely personal response to God's call. She has seen her priesthood and, therefore, her priests, as a public mediation between God and men.

They are all called to the same work for and within the community. In this sense the priesthood takes on a very public aspect. The call to the priesthood implies (in the Synod Text) a commitment both to the community of the faithful as such and also to the wider community in which the Church finds itself.[11]

The call to work, and work together, becomes the tie between priests. In the very "setting aside" of himself for God's Church the priest agrees to work with others, called in like manner, to build up God's Kingdom. When it is seen precisely as the concrete, united working out of the call to public service in the Church, the presbyterium becomes the unity of the priesthood with a specific dimension. That perspective is the priest as co-worker with his bishop and fellow-priests.

As every priest is called to work in the Church, so also is he called to the presbyterium. He functions as a member of it because his ordination gives him immediate entry into it. The call of a priest to serve Christ is at the same time an offer to work with other priests and the bishop. It is a reality that is constituted as a call to co-operation with the bishop. It is in this call that the unity of the priesthood as a function and as an office rests. The priesthood cannot be an isolated ministry even if the priest works miles from his brother priests. He does not single-handedly mediate God's grace. His call and his ministry are directed toward the sharing of a mission held by the bishop and participated in by all his fellow-priests. When he bears witness to Christ's saving death and preaches God's healing words, he does so as one who shares in a commission that no man can call his alone. The continuity of his message and the validity of his ministrations depend on his continued communion with the presbyterium. He does not in an isolated manner carry on an individually received mission. Instead he becomes part of something larger than himself. In fact, he is participating in something larger than just his personal relationship to Christ. He is a member of the presbyterium. By his call he is a priest in the Church.

The handing on of the priest's mission and ministry is done within the context of the presbyterium. No matter what a priest does, if he does it as a priest, he does it as a member of the presbyterium. When he presides at the liturgy he does so as a member of the presbyterium, as one representing the bishop. When he absolves, it is not in his own name and power that he gives healing and life: he is a representative. As a member of the body of priests, the presbyterium, he stands for the bishop. And as he stands for the bishop, he stands for the Church. And since he participates in the call of the bishop through his own ordination, he becomes a true co-worker with the bishop.

After asserting the unity of priests with the bishop and the unity of priests with each other, the Synod logically moves on to the practical expression of priestly unity.

Initially, this question concerns the type of unity the presbyterium claims for itself. On what level does the bond that holds it together operate? Is it an intrinsic and fundamental liaison which derives from the very call to the priesthood, or is it a more pragmatic alliance resting on immediate needs and responses? The answer to the question seems to be at the very bottom of the discussion on the presbyterium. The difference between the two concepts of the presbyterium is as great as that between any organic whole and a temporary working unit. The College of Bishops is an example of a theological reality that has cohesion beyond any immediate and pragmatic purpose. A political party, on the other hand, has no internal claim to life other than the service it renders its members. This distinction between organizations with an internal or integrating bond of unity and those with a merely pragmatic or external one must be applied to the presbyterium. It is either a body of priests with a specific bond that brings them together or it is only an organization with specific goals: social, political, or pastoral.

The Synod comes down in favor of the sacramental bond view of the presbyterium, as has been noted. It notes three specifics of the presbyterium: its unifying bond, its unity with the bishops, its effectiveness. Since there is a sacramental bond uniting all men in Holy Orders, the bond of priests can claim a more substantial principle of unity than mere expediency. There exists already among priests a fellowship, a brotherhood, a unity that is more than just political or social. This unifying force comes with ordination. And so any development of the notion of the presbyterium must start with the fact of ordination.

The question is one of practical means to a specific end. How do you make the presbyterium work? How do you foster cooperation between all its members? What means do you use to express the unity and function of the presbyterium in workable terms? What kind of structure will work so as to reflect as fully as possible the reality it serves?

The structure must try to provide concrete expression to the theological reality that is the presbyterium. Its function is to provide an outlet for the experiences and opinions of all the priests. Without a structure the presbyterium has no face. Without form it lacks speech. Its voice cannot be heard. And since it is a real and necessary part of the Church, it has every obligation to be heard. The Church can only profit from the experience of priests as she already does from their life and ministry.

In a sense it is through the priests' council that the presbyterium takes on flesh and blood and is able to express its opinion concretely. And as the presbyterium is made up of all the priests, each priest will have a newly articulated tie with the bishop. There will be a new visible expression of the cooperation that must exist between the two. The new structure should emphasize their cooperation in the same mission that both have received. It should highlight their common endeavor in the work of the local church. And, perhaps most importantly, its voice should bring to the local church the mature reflection of numerous experiences, points of view, and opinions derived from various ministries and pastoral activities in which the priests are involved. As a new construct, its purpose should be to facilitate the expression of the cooperation that grows out of common effort.

The ultimate criterion for the effectiveness of priests' councils will be their ability to reflect the reality they serve. They are first and foremost structures. As a construct, they are destined to serve. The reality they serve is the presbyterium. The representative priests' council seems to offer the most immediate and concrete way of giving voice to the presbyterium. Eventually the manner of their operation will vary, and new forms will develop with experience. But, as with any structure, the more clearly it mirrors the reality behind it, the more objective will be its view and the more authentic its voice.

NOTES

1. AAS, Vol. LXII, 1970, pp. 450 seq. The actual date of the circular letter is October 10, 1969.

For a study of the theology of Priests' Councils, see: Donald Wuerl, "Priests' Councils," *L'Osservatore Romano,* English Edition, No. 30 (121), July 23, 1970.

2. II, II, 1. In speaking of the activity of a Priest Council the text points out in very practical terms the central position of the bishop within the local church.

"The activity of this council cannot be fully shaped by law. Its effectiveness depends especially on a repeated effort to listen to the opinions of all in order to reach a consensus with the bishop, to whom it belongs to make the final decision."

Section 4 of Part One develops the theology of the place of the bishop within the Church. This we have referred to in Chapter Three of this book.

3. II, II, 1.
4. *Ibid.*
5. *Ibid.*
6. II, II, 2.
7. *Decree on the Bishops' Pastoral Office in the Church,* No. 28. "All priests, both diocesan and religious, participate in and exercise with the bishop the one priesthood of Christ and are thereby meant to be prudent cooperators of the episcopal order. In securing the welfare of souls, however, the first place is held by diocesan priests who are incardinated or attached to a particular church, and who fully dedicate themselves to its service by way of pasturing a single portion of the Lord's flock. In consequence, they form one presbytery and one family, whose father is the bishop. In order to distribute the sacred ministries more equitably and properly among his priests, the bishop should possess a necessary freedom in assigning offices and benefices. Therefore, rights or privileges which in any way limit this freedom are to be suppressed.

"The relationships between the bishop and his diocesan priests should rest above all upon the bonds of supernatural charity so that the harmony of the will of the priests with that of their bishop will render their pastoral activity more fruitful. Hence, for the sake of greater service to souls, let the bishop engage in discussion with his priests, even collectively, especially about pastoral matters. This he should do not only occasionally but, as far as possible, at fixed intervals."

8. *Ibid.,* No. 15: "In fulfilling their duty to sanctify, bishops should be mindful that they have been taken from among men and appointed their representatives before God in order to offer gifts and sacrifices for sins. Bishops enjoy the fullness of the sacrament of Orders, and all priests as well as deacons are dependent upon them in the exercise of authority. For the 'presbyters' are prudent fellow

workers of the episcopal order and are themselves consecrated as true priests of the New Testament, just as deacons are ordained for service and minister to the People of God in communion with the bishop and his presbytery. Therefore bishops are the principal dispensers of the mysteries of God, just as they are the governors, promoters, and guardians of the entire liturgical life in the church committed to them."

9. *Ibid.,* No. 28.

10. *Ibid.,* No. 15 and 28 and *Decree on the Ministry and Life of Priests,* No. 2.

"So it was that Christ sent the apostles just as he himself had been sent by the Father. Through these same apostles he made their successors, the bishops, sharers in his consecration and mission. Their ministerial role has been handed down to priests in a limited degree. Thus established in the order of the priesthood, they are co-workers of the episcopal order in the proper fulfillment of the apostolic mission entrusted to the latter order by Christ.

"Inasmuch as it is connected with the episcopal order, the priestly office shares in the authority by which Christ himself builds up, sanctifies, and rules his body. Therefore, while it indeed presupposes the sacraments of Christian initiation, the sacerdotal office of priests is conferred by that special sacrament through which priests, by the anointing of the Holy Spirit, are marked with a special character and are so configured to Christ the Priest that they can act in the person of Christ the Head."

11. "The proper mission entrusted by Christ to the priest, as to the Church, is not of the political, economic or social order, but of the religious order (*cf.* GS 42); yet, in the pursuit of his ministry, the priest can contribute greatly to the establishment of a more just secular order, especially in places where the human problems of injustice and oppression are more serious. He must always, however, preserve ecclesial communion and reject violence in words or deeds as not being in accordance with the gospel.

"In fact, the word of the gospel which he proclaims in the name of Christ and the Church, and the effective grace of sacramental life which he administers should free man from his personal and social egoism and foster among men conditions of justice, which would be a sign of the love of Christ present among us (*cf.* GS 58)." I, I, 7.

9. *Permanence of the Priesthood*

ONE OF THE corollaries that follow on the Synod's doctrine of the priesthood as a participation in the mission of Christ is its view on the permanence of the priesthood. The Synod sees in the "laying on of hands" the communication of a "gift of the Holy Spirit that cannot be lost." The theological supposition for the statement is that the priest through Orders is "configured" to Christ. The priest is made one with Christ and his mission.

"By the laying on of hands there is communicated a gift of the Holy Spirit which can not be lost (*cf*: 2 Tm 1:6). This reality configures the ordained minister to Christ the Priest, consecrates him (*cf.* P.O. No. 2) and makes him a sharer in Christ's mission under its two aspects of authority and service."[1]

Since he is one with Christ, he becomes to all the Christian community a "pledge of the salvific presence of Christ." He becomes in an "irrevocable" way associated with the Church as Christ is.

"The minister whose life bears the seal of the gift received through the sacrament of Orders reminds the Church that the gift of God is irrevocable. In the midst of the Christian community which in spite of its defects lives by the Spirit, he is a pledge of the salvific presence of Christ."[2]

He shares in the mission of Christ. And as the mission is "ongoing," the priest's part in the eschatological work of reconciliation "is," by implication, "continuous."[3] As the man is joined to Christ and his mission, and as that mission is yet to be completed, his commission must be permanent.

This line of logic seems based on the idea that the priest *is* a priest by reason of his identification with Christ and his works. If the work, the mission, is ongoing, the identity with it is continuous. The priest's selection was in terms of his continuous witness to an eschatological event. As his participation in the mission is according to the power of Christ to bring about the eschatological work of reconciliation, so the priestly consecration implies an eschatological dedication and mission that must be permanent and enduring. To attempt a part-time short-term manifestation of Christ's eschatological work is a contradiction.

The Synod sees priestly dedication and consecration against the backdrop of Christ's authority and work, both of which are to find their recognition and completion in the day of the fulfillment of the Kingdom.

"That authority does not belong to the minister as his own: it is a manifestation of the 'exousia' (i.e., the power) of the Lord, by which the priest is an ambassador of Christ in the eschatological work of reconciliation (*cf.* 2 Cor 5:18–20). He also assists the conversion of human freedom to God for the building up of the Christian community."[4]

Once the priest is ordained and starts to function with the "authority" of God, he becomes a manifestation of God's power in this world. That manifestation depends on God and cannot be turned on and off by the priest even if he chooses to leave the active ministry.

"This special participation in Christ's priesthood does not disappear even if a priest . . . is dispensed or removed from the exercise of his ministry."[5]

The Synod also sees ordination as an eschatological sign of the finality of Christ's Kingdom. The supposition behind this statement is the Church's conviction that all men are actively to bring about the reign and triumph of Christ's Kingdom through their own conversion to it. This conversion includes the will and mind. The priest's free giving of himself prefigures the day when Christ's Kingdom will reign in fullness. In that Kingdom all will freely give themselves to Christ in a manner that will admit of no reversal. In his act of acceptance of priestly orders the priest "assists the conversion of human freedom to God" by stepping forever into the world of union with Christ in faith and grace.[6] This world or Kingdom, mirrored faintly now, will one day burst out in full glory when Christ's reconciliation is complete. In the meantime, the priest must remain a sign of the Kingdom to come and be "a pledge of the salvific presence of Christ."

"The lifelong permanence of this reality, which is a sign, and which is a teaching of the faith and is referred to in the Church's tradition as the priestly character, expresses the fact that Christ associated the Church with himself in an irrevocable way for the salvation of the world, and that the Church dedicates herself to Christ in a definitive way for the carrying out of his work. The minister whose life bears the seal of the gift received through the sacrament of Orders reminds the Church that the gift of God is irrevocable. In the midst of the Christian community which, in spite of its defects, lives by the Spirit, he is a pledge of the salvific presence of Christ."[7]

Since the priest is configured to Christ, his priesthood is in some way a permanent part of his being. How this comes to pass is not explained in the document. But the traditional manner of expressing the lifelong permanence of the reality is repeated and confirmed. A "priestly character" is in some way introduced into the life and being of the priest. Its purpose is to express the fact that "Christ associated the Church with himself in an irrevocable way for the salvation of the world."[8]

The means chosen to confer the "seal" is to confirm the priest in the Holy Spirit and make of him a visible "pledge of the salvific presence of Christ."[9]

The priesthood, following this view, is not just for the service of God's people at this stage of the development of the Kingdom: it exists also to reflect the permanent and transcendent union of Christ with his Kingdom and to be a sign of the eschatological fulfillment of the Kingdom according to Christ's wish. In this sense, the eschatological nature of the priesthood touches every aspect of the priest's work and life. When the document speaks of permanence in the priesthood under this eschatological aspect, it sees the subject as both an ontological and functional reality. The priest is configured to Christ in a manner that affects his being. The "reality" of union with Christ is expressed in what is called a "character." It exists for the specific purpose of relating the priest's eschatological function to the world. Through it, the permanent salvific presence of Christ is to be prefigured and made in some way present.

This "character" must be related to the other sacraments, for they do precisely what the document attributes to the priestly "character." All the sacraments attempt to make Christ present in this world — though in a limited and imperfect way; they are all pointing forward to a perfection which is not yet accomplished. In the priesthood, the eschatological element is the priest's representation of Christ's eternal salvific action of redemption. The indication of this priestly eschatological function is seen in the document as priestly "character." It signifies the permanence of Christ's priestly redemptive work as it is found in this world in the exercise of Sacred Orders.

Priestly character then is not merely a designation of office "imprinted on the soul." It is not a new badge of the insignia of a rank. It is an ontological expression of the breakthrough into this world of the redemptive power of Christ. As such, it is both a sign and an effective means of Christ's presence.

This seems to explain why the document first of all declares the priesthood to be a "consecration" that is "irrevocable," and then extends the priestly ministry into the eschatological realm of the Kingdom yet to come. The document sees identification of the priest with Christ as a union so intimate that the priest's very being is altered. Hence the document's reference to a "character" imprinted on the soul to indicate the supernatural union of the priest with Christ.

Only in the eschatological order can the "character" as expressed in the Synod be fully explained: only within that order can certain realities which lie beyond our limited human experience be represented and effected. As Karl Rahner notes:

"It is not an anticipatory reporting of events that are to happen 'later' but the prospective view — necessary for man with his spiritual freedom of decision — from his present situation in saving history, governed by the event of Christ, to the final fulfillment of this his own existential situation, which is really already eschatologically determined."[10]

This is the scope of the sacraments; this is the function of the Eucharist and Sacred Orders, of which the eschatological aspect is the "once and for all permanent"[11] aspect of redemption in the New Covenant. The Synod places the discussion of the "character" here because it sees it as the "sign . . . that Christ associated the Church with himself in an irrevocable way."[12] There is no turning back for the Church. She is irrevocably committed to Christ. The priest's special calling and consecration reflects this fact of faith. His "priestly character" is a permanent sign and reminder of the permanence of Christ's redemptive union with the Church and her irrevocable communion with Him.

The document draws another conclusion from the permanence of priestly Orders. In the section on the spiritual life of priests, it reminds priests that "like the apostles they share in a special way" companionship with Christ. This companionship must express itself in the zeal for souls because "there can be no dichotomy between love for Christ and zeal for souls."[13]

"Just as Christ, anointed by the Holy Spirit, was impelled by his deep love for his Father and gave his life for men, so the priest, consecrated by the Holy Spirit, and in a special way made like to Christ the Priest, dedicates himself to the work of the Father performed through the Son. Thus the whole rule for the priest's life is expressed in the words of Jesus: 'And for their sake I consecrate myself, that they also may be consecrated in truth' (Jn 17:19)."[14]

The eschatological aspect of the priesthood is also applied by the Synod to the question of celibacy. Perhaps even more explicitly, the section on celibacy notes the representation in this world of absolutes in anticipation of their full consummation in the Kingdom of God.

"Within modern culture, in which spiritual values are to a great extent obscured, the celibate priest indicates the presence of the Absolute God, who invites us to be renewed in his image. Where the value of sexuality is so exaggerated that genuine love is forgotten, celibacy for the sake of the Kingdom of Christ calls men back to the sublimity of faithful love and reveals the ultimate meaning of life.

"Furthermore, one rightly speaks of the value of celibacy as an eschatological sign. By transcending every contingent human value, the celibate priest associates himself in a special way with Christ as the final and absolute good and shows forth, in anticipation, the freedom of the children of God. While the value of the sign and holiness of Christian marriage is fully recognized, celibacy for the sake of the Kingdom nevertheless more clearly displays that spiritual fruitfulness or generative power of the New Law by which the apostle knows that in Christ he is the father and mother of his communities."[15]

In summary, it seems that the document's reflection on the permanence of the priesthood rests on the theological principle that the priest in his ordination is united to Christ. This union is articulated in the priest's participation in the mission of Christ. The mission of Christ will find its completion only in the days of the glory of God's Kingdom. Until that time, the priest remains the living sign of the present kingdom and the promise of its completion in glory.

Both the priesthood and the witness to the coming perfection of the Kingdom of God share a permanence that emanates from Christ's one and final revelation and his irrevocable union with his Church. Neither the Church nor the priesthood as its functioning sign can cease to be. They remain in this world the expression of the permanence of Christ so that the priest becomes an "ambassador of Christ in the eschatological work of reconciliation."[16]

NOTES

1. I, 5.
2. *Ibid.*
3. *Ibid.*
4. *Ibid.*
5. *Ibid.*
6. *Ibid.*
7. *Ibid.*
8. *Ibid.*
9. *Ibid.*
10. Rahner, p. 149.
11. Rahner, p. 71: "The doctrine was first developed by St. Augustine on the basis of the recognized fact that none of these sacraments could be repeated. The indelibility of the sacramental character places it beyond the sphere of human decision."
12. I, 5.
13. II, I, 3.
14. *Ibid.*
15. II, I, 4.
16. I, 5.

10. *The Hierarchical Church*

According to divine plan, the Church is hierarchical, divided into bishops, priests, deacons, and laity. As we have seen, Christ's mission is not parcelled out, as it were, among his followers. It is shared by all. Some, however, are called through the sacrament of Orders to participate in a special way in the mission. The essence of this special participation is found in the sacrament of Holy Orders.

Perhaps one of the ways to see what the Synod taught and teaches is to compare it with the writing of someone who has a different view of Orders and of the development of the priesthood within the Church. In making such a comparison, the teaching of the Synod becomes clear by contrast. One such background against which to study the Church's teaching is the recently popular work of Hans Küng, *Why Priests?*[1] Küng is presenting — as a theologian and in theological terms — a complete set of conclusions that are based on his own ecclesiology. He is offering an alternative view of the Church and therefore of its ministries according to the theological terms that he accepts and following the epistomological device he favors.

The theological system of Küng sees the Church as essentially "pneumatic and charismatic in structure."[2] He discards, according to one generally accepted reading of his works, "the sacramental structure and levels the hierarchical community to a Church which is in all its ground functions one communion in freedom, equality, and fraternity."[3] Within this framework he discusses the priesthood, since as a ministry it must somehow find its place in the democratic church that Küng's system proposes.

In *Why Priests?* Küng explains his theory of the development of the traditional conception of the office of priest within the Church.[4] To put it briefly, he sees the office of priest and bishop as later developments that were heavily influenced by an adjustment of the structures of ecclesial service to that of the Roman civil service.[5] Within this system, the episcopate, presbyterate, and diaconate were henceforth considered to be obligatory ministerial structures imparted by the laying on of hands and prayers.[6] The fuller "sacralization and ritualization" of these offices came in the fifth and sixth centuries.[7]

Küng reserves to the Middle Ages the development of the "sacramental conception" of priestly ministry, and concludes his historical survey by attributing relativity to the elements in the development of the traditional priesthood.[8] With such a description of the historical evolution of the priesthood and the general absence of functional continuity with apostolic times, it is not surprising that Küng asserts both that the traditional priesthood can never claim the normative value of origins, and that there can be no decisive objections on such grounds to a new conception and a renewed form of the ministry of leadership in the Church.

Having disposed of the classical theological basis for the traditional Catholic concept of the ministerial priesthood, Küng feels free to design and outline a wholly new priesthood which takes as its principle of departure the need for leadership. The decision to re-define and restructure the priesthood, since no normative concept of priesthood is exclusively authentic, seems to indicate just how much force Küng gives to the word "development" when he does his historical research and arrives at his conclusions. The word, as he uses it, has all the force of "invention" or "additional" rather than "unfolding."

In a review of Küng's works, Fr. Raymond Brown writes that:

"Küng the architect of Church reform plays the most prominent role in this book. His theses echo like hammer blows on Mother Church's door. The Christian needs no priest as a mediator with God; any special priesthood has been dissolved by the priesthood of Christ; authority in the Church is legitimate only if based on service and not on power; both 'priest' and 'hierarchy' should be dropped from our vocabulary; special ministry in the Church need not be full-time or lifetime or academically trained or male or celibate; ordination does not give an ordinand an entitive character distinguishing him from the layman and empowering him to administer the Eucharist, for all Christians have that power."[9]

The Synod faces the question of the origin of the priesthood in terms of its function, as has been repeatedly noted. From such a starting point it is concerned with the ministry or ministries that participate in the functions of Christ, as Priest, Prophet and King.[10] The emphasis of the Synod is not on the historical, cultural or social influences that colored and formed the style and mood of the expression of priestly office within the Church. For the Synod, the apostolic Church in the person of the apostles, their successors and their "helpers in the ministry" carried on from the beginning the mission of Christ. By locating the definition of the priesthood in the person of Christ and his works, the Synod prescinds from the historical coloring of the trappings of office. The theological justification for such an approach seems to be the document's acceptance of the incarnational imperative that any mission needs to be clothed in the cloth of the day. Christ's own acceptance of the human condition sets the premise for the Church's incarnational and existential self view.

The Council document[11] on which the Synod relies points out the continuity of Christ's mission with that of the Church and the parallel between the manners in which both approach the task.

"The Son . . . came on mission from the Father. It was in him, before the foundation of the world, that the Father chose and predestined us to become adopted sons . . . To carry out the will of the Father Christ inaugurated the Kingdom of heaven on earth and revealed the mystery of the Father," No. 3.
"When the work which the Father had given the Son to do on

earth (*cf.* Jn 17:4) was accomplished, the Holy Spirit was sent . . . that he might forever sanctify the Church, and thus all believers would have access to the Father through Christ . . ." No. 4. "In Christ's word, in his works and in his presence this Kingdom reveals itself to men" No. 5.

The teaching of the Council document is one that

includes an understanding of how Christ is in relation to his Church. He is tied to it since he founded it and made it his Kingdom, already present in a mysterious way. It becomes the work of that same Church to announce and extend the Kingdom here on earth and in this way to initiate in itself the final Kingdom which will be realized in glory at the end of time.

The means used by Christ, his Incarnation, to reach men are paralleled in the Church by her "sacramental" nature, by which she is a sign and instrument visibly manifesting in a limited way her full power and mysterious glory.

What the Synod seems to be accepting as a starting point is that the essential priesthood has existed and does exist in the continuity of the functions that the priest performs. These functions are an extension in time and space of the priestly action of Christ and as such existed from the beginning of the Church. A further development of this doctrine is the Church's insistence that she herself is a sacrament — *the* sacrament — that continues to make Christ and his work present.

By concentrating on the function of the priest, the Synod defines the priesthood in terms of the work of Christ that his ministers have from the beginning carried out. The document does not deny that certain clarifications were worked out in time. Nor does it refuse to accept that at times, the priest, while exercising his functions, may have taken on various titles and related formal obligations. However, the Synod does not see in this existential incarnational situation of the priesthood a denial that the essential functions of the priest are constantly and continually performed as they were in the beginning, notwithstanding any cultural influences on the priest.

An argument can be made — but this is not in the Synod's text, which is not addressed to the problem of the cultural development of the priestly office — that accretions to the visible manifestation of that office were the result of the recognition by the believing community of the priest's unique office and function. Rather than see in his cultural development an addition to his self-understanding as a priest, we might say that the additions to the priest's visible office followed on the general recognition of his functional status. The Synod seems only to concentrate on the essential work of participation in the mission of Christ that the priest enjoys in a specific manner. This specifically differentiated ministry, so the documents states, pertains to the original structure of the Church.

In this view of the priesthood — which accepts a picture of the Church in which the apostles handed on to others the powers entrusted to them in so far as they were communicable, and in which these others were obliged to hand them on to yet others — the priest is seen not in his name nor in his assumption of administrative and organization duties, but in the mission in which he participates.

There seems to be a very real difference between Küng's view of the priest and that of the Synod. The fundamental difference seems to be located in the prior understanding of the nature of the Church. For Küng, the primitive Church, with the apostles and others teaching with authority and making Christ present by their powers, is already an alien one — at least alien to his interpretation of Scripture.

As we have pointed out, Küng's exegesis is not without challenge. Brown calls it into question in his review of Küng's works in *America*:

"As I pointed out in *Priest and Bishop,* Küng's exegesis is often minimalistic and hypercritical. For instance, there is no real *New Testament* evidence for Küng's insistent relating of the celebration of the Eucharist to the priesthood of the faithful."[12]

His system places the "basic apostolic succession" in the Church in general and individually only in each member of the Church.[13] However, without some sort of differentiated mission in the primitive Church, there can be none in any later age. And by locating all apostolic succession in the Church in general and not in individuals, Küng has eliminated the foundation for any type of differentiation other than nominal within the Christian community.

If one accepts the original premise of Küng in his understanding of the Church, then any clarification of the priestly ministry has to be seen as a later addition to the life and structure of the Church. For if no structure existed or was part of the primitive Church, then any development of one is essentially an addition. This general elimination of any essential differentiality of the apostolic mission is obviously hard to reconcile with the Synod's text that "the twelve apostles . . . passed on to their immediate cooperators" not only duties but powers.

Lawlor supports this interpretation of Küng and the difficulties it presents:

"This across the board homogenization of the apostolicity and of the collegiality of the Church, with its elimination of any essential concentration of the apostolic mission, sacramentally conferred and carried on in the episcopal college as such, obviously shunts aside the doctrine of the apostolic succession of the episcopal college and 'dismisses the essential difference' which Vatican II says (LG 10) exists between the ordained priesthood and the common priesthood of the baptized. 'The ministerial priest, in virtue of the sacred power which is his, forms and rules the priestly people' (LG 10)."[14]

Lawlor continues his analysis of the ecclesiology found in the writings of Küng. He finds a Church which is without distinction of any sort:

"As I read it, Küng's ecclesiology desacramentalizes the Church as such. The mystery of the total Church as unitary communion in the life, mission, and destiny of Christ is undermined by two pervasive orientations of his ecclesiology, namely, by its individualism and its extrinsicism. For reasons of space, only the individualistic orientation will be considered in this article.

"In Küng's system the Church as such does not present itself as an organic totality. Rather it appears as an aggregate or assemblage of believing individuals, in each one of whom a rudimentary but essential churchliness is verified."[15]

Küng bases his assertion on his interpretation of the historical development within the Church of its full understanding of the nature of the priesthood. However, given his conclusions, we must conclude that Küng has an idiosyncratic understanding of "development." We are forced to read for "development," in his writing, not "clarification" and "stabilization" in the traditional theological sense, but "adaptation" and "addition." When speaking of the priesthood, Küng's initial premise leads us to see in the historical development of the patterns of priestly ministry a gradual addition to the Church of a new office and function. In addition, given his premise that the Church is a communion in liberty, equality and fraternity and his application of these terms, there is no room for a hierarchy even of service that is more than nominal. His definition of liberty within the Church,[16] equality of believers[17] and the brotherhood of the faith[18] leaves no room for any type of ministry that could claim authority from any source.

Not only does Küng's consideration of ministerial differentiation within the apostolic Church lead to conclusions different from those of the Synod, but his appreciation of the function of the priesthood in particular presents a contrast to that of the Synod's document. When we turn to the priest in Küng's book, we read:

"Today it is less easy than ever to make out the essence of the ecclesial office . . . to tell the truth no one any longer knows what is a 'priest' or 'bishop' and for what reason he is a 'priest' or 'bishop.' "[19]

In essence, the priest, as Küng sees him, is called to a leadership of service that, however, does not carry with it any specific function that is not also a function performable by any other believer. In fact, ordination is merely a temporary designation and applicable to all sorts of activities ranging from catechist to social worker.

Küng points out a view of priestly ministry that considers it "not necessarily a life-long task"[20] but rather a "service that would be a second profession."[21] It could be accepted for a specific duration of time and then relinquished. In view of this understanding of priestly ordination, it is not surprising that we find that the rest of the section dealing with this subject in Küng's work is entitled "Variables of the Ministry of Leadership"[22] and deals exclusively with the various present-day ecclesial practices that could be abandoned by the Church if she were to accept this view of the priesthood. There would be no further need for university training,[23] theological preparation,[24] celibacy,[25] or the exclusion of women from the priesthood.[26] All these conclusions follow from an assertion of a non-permanent priestly ministry, an assertion that a permanent ministry is obsolete, that any such calling can only be temporary.

When Küng's ecclesiology and his view of mission are blended, it becomes nearly impossible to define exactly what is a specifically priestly ministry. Given his view of the "democratic" Church, Küng is unable to assign functions to his newly-created "priest," since his Church is a company of essentially equal believers in whom the various charismatic ministries are all Spirit-evoked, authorized, and confirmed, and among whom there is at work a reciprocity of services on the part of all for all. In this Church "each member freely honors and submits to the charism proper to every other" and hence there is no need for a structured hierarchy even of service.[27] Küng is confined to presenting a ministry of leadership which claims no specific function and rests at the total disposition of the community in the sense of a spiritual orientation.[28]

Küng's position seems rooted in his denying that the Church has recognized and continues to recognize in the priest a disciple set apart and called to represent Christ in a fuller way to the community of believers, and that it is the imposition of hands which renders the priest a sharer in the priesthood of Christ, in a manner that differentiates him from the rest of the community. This leads him to describe the function of a priest as a temporary one, since it is considered not as a consecration and union with Christ but an expression of a designation by the community to perform a certain temporary duty that could just as well be performed by another.

The Synod when speaking of the permanence of the priesthood links it to the communication of the Holy Spirit which makes the priest uniquely one with Christ and which is a gift that cannot be lost. The priest is to be a permanent witness to the eschatological victory of Christ and the permanence and completeness of his victory over the world and death. Again the root of the difference seems to be in the understanding of the meaning of function in relationship to the priestly participation in the mission of Christ. The Synod uses the term to mean a share in the intrinsic mission that was Christ's. To function as did Christ does not mean to perform the outward work he did. It means to enter into the mandate and mission Christ received from his Father. Such a participation identifies the priest not just with the outward function that bears a similarity to that of Christ but to the very person and radical mission of the Lord.

Küng, while speaking of function and ministry, repeatedly appeals to the exercise of these functions as if they were transient works not of Christ manifested in the priest but the work of the community which from time to time needs someone to perform certain duties.

Perhaps here we can see a more fundamental difference between Küng and the Synod. The Synod relies on the existential incarnational view of the Church as that sacrament of Christ and his presence which is operative in the priests. The formula that sees Christ handing on to his apostles his gift and the apostles in turn handing on what they received includes the existential view of specific real flesh and blood individuals receiving their mission and placing themselves at the disposition of the Church. The Church receives from Christ, in the person of those who carry on her work, the power to actualize his work. It seems that this view takes into account the limited manner of the Church's sacramental existence and accounts for the need that the Church act in a human fashion to reach the believer who still lives on this earth and is taken up with the limitations of this life. Küng's position seems to ignore the radical limitations of the incarnational Church and to opt for a Church somehow perfect in the Lord because of the sovereignty of the Spirit in the charismatic life of the community and the obedience of all the faithful to the Spirit, together with a mutual charity in the exercise of all charismatic ministries which eliminate all tension and confrontation. This vision of the Church, however, does not seem to be verifiable in fact and is repudiated by Küng in his own claim that the real historical Church is a sinful one. Lawlor challenges the "pneumatic utopianism" of Küng precisely in terms of Küng's monotonous claim that the real Church is a "sinful Church." He continues that "one would have to be a believer in a fully realized eschatology in order to give credit to such a solution."[29]

Küng speaks of the ministry of leadership as a "permanent service in the Christian Community."[30] But since this ministry is primarily ecclesial and social and not sacramental, it need not be localized in any one person set aside to accept the mission. Rather the Church accepts the mission, and in the Church, every service of leadership, "whether institutionalized or not by the laying on of hands, presupposes a link with the first witness and first mission of the apostles."[31] Therefore, all believers, according to Küng, participate directly in the mission of Christ because they share in the mission of the Church. The actualization of the powers given to the Church by Christ is not determined by any consecrated differentiation within the community of believers but immediately by the community itself.

The Synod's view is quite different on this point. It sees the Church as the principal mediator of Christ in the world. But it recognizes that the actualization of the powers and mission of the Church as the body of Christ is through special people within the community. The Synod's premise seems to include the practical existential matter of how concretely the Church of Christ carries out her mandate while still in the world. The document claims that Christ's choice of specific followers to continue his particular work is the foundation of a hierarchical system that carries on Christ's work in his chosen way.

Küng's position, as it is represented in sections 3 and 4 of chapter 4, seems to be that the Church as the unstructured body of believers shares in Christ's mission and actualizes that work by the charismatic activity of individuals, who can exercise the fullness of the powers left the Church by Christ by the simple and temporary designation of them to do so by the same unstructured Church. In this manner, permanent orders are not needed. They would not reflect the democratic nature of the Christian community.

It is not hard to see that there is some clash between the position of Küng and that of the Synod. Brown notes the difficulty of reconciling the traditional teaching and Küng's. This he finds the result of Küng's major theological premise which "involves the democratization of the Church and the reshaping of ministerial roles."

"If the current mode of priestly ministry is a fixed part of a blueprint that Christ gave to the apostles for the Church, obviously there is little room for the changes Küng envisions. Consequently his crucial theological concern is with apostolic succession."[32]

Since one is a theological interpretation of historical and scriptural data and the other is a magisterial statement on a doctrinal subject, there is still great room theoretically for a clarification of seeming or real divergencies. However, in the case of Küng's work, several assertions seem to challenge the very foundation of the statement by the Synod. The most formidable assertion of such wide-ranging implication is the explicit rejection of a hierarchical structure within the Church. This position renders the discussion of ordination, specific function and priestly ministry sterile by denying the premise from which such a discussion would depart. Küng's position, as we have noted, is that there is no permanently established differentiation of ministries within the Church. No individual is selected to carry on the specific function of Christ's mission. The community is the only permanent entity of residual sacred mission. At this point we find a major disagreement with the Synod's position. It sees the continuity of residual powers expressed concretely in the ordination by the Church of certain members who will hereafter act in a way particularly identified with Christ and share in his authority. The matter seems to boil down to the "how" of the actualization within the Church of the manifest power to represent Christ. Küng's reply offers a general orientation of the Church expressed in temporary charismatic formulations. The Synod opts for a concrete actualization and continuity in the order of priest for the mission of Christ in his Church.

Another essential point at issue is that of development. Küng cites the legitimate development of the concept of priestly ordination, but also states that it is an addition to the Church's operational attitude and not "instituted by Christ." By contrast, the Synod asserts that the priestly office is of apostolic origin stemming from the mandate of Christ. If it means (as implied by Küng) "addition," then we find the priesthood to be an accretion — "wholly legitimate" and "not an instance of degeneration" but nonetheless an addition to the Church as Christ founded it. If we follow the Synod's view of function with the apostolic community seen as the work of Christ continued, then the stabilization of this work through an ordination ceremony is not an "addition" but a clarification of an already existing mandate, mission, and concrete office of actualization.

NOTES

1. See note one Introduction.
2. *Die Kirche* (Freiburg: Herder, 1967). For the English translation of quotations used here we will cite the translation of Ray and Rosaleen Ockenden, *The Church* (London: Burns & Oates, 1968), pp. 150-202.
3. Francis Lawlor, "Laity and Clergy According to Küng," *Homiletic and Pastoral Review,* Vol. LXXIII, No. 7, July 1973, p. 10.

For a theological dialogue in which the position of Küng is made clear, see the Rahner-Küng debate in the *Homiletic and Pastoral Review,* Vol. LXXI, Nos. 8, 9, 10 and 11.

4. Küng, Chapter Three, pp. 37-51.
5. *Ibid.,* p. 37. "The structure of ecclesial service was (significantly) adjusted to that of the Roman civil service, with its *'ordines'*: services arranged as finely gradated *'offices.'* The bishop became a high functionary administering a territory, with presbyters, deacons, and other ministers of the church as his subordinates."
6. *Ibid.,* p. 38. "Despite the existence of other ecclesial functions, which allowed room for a greater degree of flexibility, the *episcopate, presbyterate* and *diaconate* were henceforth considered to be the obligatory ministerial structure, imparted by the laying-on of hands and by prayers."
7. *Ibid.* This interpretation of Küng is confirmed in the article on Küng found in the "Ampleforth Journal," Vol. LXXIII, Part II, Summer, 1968, p. 220. "Hans Küng has made his position clear in his new book, 'The Church' (to be reviewed in the next JOURNAL by Rev. A.M. Allchin), esp. D.IV.2 and E.II.2. The point is crystallized in his article 'What is the Essence of Apostolic Succession?' in

Concilium IV, 4, 16–19 (April 1968). There he says that 'the whole Church and every individual member share in the apostolic succession: the Church as a whole is committed to obedience to the apostles as the original witnesses . . . the concept suffers from a clerical narrowing down if this apostolic succession is seen exclusively as a succession of ecclesiastical functions . . . it is the Church as a whole that we believe in. The Church as a whole is successor to the apostles . . . every individual member stands in this apostolic succession. Every later generation remains bound to the word, the witness, and the service of the first apostolic generation . . . Apostolic succession is therefore primarily a succession in apostolic faith, apostolic service, and apostolic life. It is a juridical narrowing of the concept to see apostolic succession primarily in a continuous chain of impositions of hands. As if such a chain of ordinations could supply by itself the apostolic spirit! The point of the succession lies in the constantly renewed daily loyalty to the apostles.' He shows that the three-fold order of functions (bishop, priest, and deacon) which St. Ignatius of Antioch discusses in the second century, while it is rooted in the customs of the apostolic Church, nevertheless 'can simply not be identified as a whole original order and distribution of all the functions. It is the result of a very complex historical development! So even the first link of the pipe is not merely one link."

8. *Ibid.*, p. 39. "For a theological, and therefore practical, understanding of ecclesial service, the *sacramental conception* of this ministry, which dates from the Middle Ages (but, in fact, has its origins in patristic times) is significant. With the researchers of the high Middle Ages into the concept of a sacrament and with the process of reflection that gradually produced the seven sacraments in the twelfth and thirteenth centuries, it was necessary to define precisely the sacramental nature of ecclesial ordination — a sacramentality concentrated on the presbyterate."

9. Raymond Brown, "The Changing Face of the Priesthood," *America,* May 20, 1973, p. 531.

10. I, 4.

11. The *Dogmatic Constitution on the Church,* Nos. 3, 4 and 5.

12. Brown, *America,* p. 531.

13. Küng, p. 31: "The apostolic succession is primarily a succession to the faith and creed of the apostles and to the apostolic service and life."

P. 33: "The apostolic mission and apostolic service were still necessary. Both were assumed by the Church as a whole, which, as a whole, can and should remain the 'Ecclesia apostolica.'"

14. "Some Thoughts on Küng's Ecclesiology," *Homiletic and Pastoral Review,* Vol. LXXIII, No. 4, January 1973, pp. 10–20, esp.

p. 15.

15. *Ibid.*, p. 11.

16. Küng, p. 20: "The Church itself should be both the *location of liberty* and the *advocate of liberty in the world.*

"In such a community of free individuals, all members without distinction would then be able, thanks to the light and power of Jesus, to retain their liberty in the world of today, despite its constraints (the slavery of the economy, of science, of the state), despite 'idols' (the personality cult) and false gods (the worship of riches, pleasure and power)."

17. *Ibid.*, pp. 21:24: "On the basis of a given and realized liberty, the Church will (as it can and must) be a *community of fundamentally equal individuals.*"

18. *Ibid.*, pp. 23, 24: "On the basis of a given and actual liberty and equality, the Church can and ought to be a community of brothers and sisters. Commissioned by Jesus Christ, the Church as an institution must never use the patriarchal form of government."

19. *Ibid.*, p. 52.
20. *Ibid.*, p. 55.
21. *Ibid.*, p. 54.
22. *Ibid.*, p. 52.
23. *Ibid.*, p. 56.
24. *Ibid.*, p. 57.
25. *Ibid.*, pp. 57–59.
26. *Ibid.*, pp. 59, 60.
27. Lawlor, p. 14.
28. Küng, p. 60.
29. Lawlor, p. 13.
30. Küng, p. 60.
31. *Ibid.*, p. 63.
32. Brown, *America,* p. 513.

11. The Priest in Sacred Scripture

THE SACRAMENT OF Holy Orders is rooted in the selection of the first bishops — the apostles — and the apostolic succession which began at that point.

Of course, there are questions that come up when one begins to interpret what is meant by the apostolic succession or hierarchy in the Church. Father Raymond Brown, S.S., in his work *Priest and Bishop: Biblical Reflections* offers some exegetical points that help us in the study of what is meant by apostolic succession. We will use his work as a background against which to see what the Synod said about this same point.

Clearly the Synod's position on apostolic succession is that the bishops are to the Church today what the apostles were to the primitive Christian community.

"They [the apostles] appointed such men and made provision that, when these men should die, other appointed men would take up their ministry."[1]

The Synod document refers to the more detailed statement of this doctrine found in the Council.

"For they not only had helpers in their ministry, but also, in order that the mission assigned to them might continue after their death, they passed on to their immediate cooperators, as a kind of testament, the duty of perfecting and consolidating the work begun by themselves, charging them to attend to the whole flock in which the Holy Spirit placed them to shepherd the Church of God (*cf.* Acts 20:28). They therefore appointed such men, and authorized the arrangement that, when these men should have died, other approved men would take up their ministry."[2]

Because the bishop cannot reach all those committed to his care, he shares his priestly order with others on a "subordinate level."[3] These "others" are the priests — known as such in the Church today, as they have been so recognized from the beginning. The priesthood in this view is a hierarchical participation in the sacrament of Orders which has existed from the begining in the Church and is necessary for its continuing life.[4]

The synodal document supports its theological and doctrinal conclusions with an interpretation of Sacred Scripture. In this section the principal assertions which the Synod sees confirmed in the New Testament are:

1. The relationship of apostle to community as head

to body belongs to the "original inalienable structure of the Church."[5]

2. The extension of the work of the apostles was through "helpers in their ministry."[6]
3. The continuation of the work of the apostles is found in their successors, the bishops.[7]
4. The continuation in the shared mission of the bishops is found in the subordinate level of Orders, the priesthood.[8]
5. The notion of permanency in the priesthood is tied to the priestly consecration that one receives by the laying on of hands.[9]

In the first chapter of his work *Priest and Bishop: Biblical Reflections,* Brown explores some of the biblical background of the Catholic priesthood. He reaches some theological conclusions that contrast in part with those of the Synod. We will try here to set forth some of those conclusions linked with his exegetical premises. In this way we hope to shed some light on the purpose and import of the synodal document and its doctrine.

Brown concludes that the priest as he is identified today is not so easily recognized in the pages of the New Testament. For example, he indicates that the identification of the priest as the one who exclusively presided at the Eucharist is not established in the New Testament. The formal priesthood is seen by Brown as the "combination or distillation of several distinct roles and special ministries in the NT Church."[10] This conclusion rests on the exegetical premise that "no individual Christian is ever specifically identified as a priest."[11] He continues that the ministry of the NT is not confined to presidency at the Eucharistic meal. The exclusive right of the priest to preside at the Eucharist was not recognized in the NT Church. Brown therefore concludes that the theological view of the priesthood as an exclusive ministry and order, with the unique power of the sacramental ministry of the Eucharist, is a later development within the Church.[12]

The idea of a specific priesthood which was connected intrinsically with the Eucharist, Brown continues, had to await a certain development or maturing within the Christian community. This maturing consisted in an understanding of the Christian way as distinct from the Jewish religion.[13] Then the community had to come to see the Eucharist as sacrifice. Only when the notion of priesthood and Eucharistic sacrifice were used side by side can we speak of a priesthood in the Church understood as it is today. This union of ideas, for Brown, took place towards the end of the first century or the beginning of the second.[14]

Within this view of the early Church and its ministries, the existence of the substance of the priesthood is not denied. Brown does not state that no ministry of orders functioned within the primitive Church. On the contrary, he sees several different ministries carrying on work in a somewhat undefined manner. Part of the "work" thus performed includes those functions later spoken of as uniquely priestly actions.

It seems important to note that Brown's view of a gradual development or clarification of priestly functions does not mean that such functions came into being later in the life of the Church. He is pointing out that the designation by specific names of particular functions and functionaries developed later — and not all that later — in the life of the Church. When one states that the designation of a particular order to perform a specific sacrificial office required time and self-understanding, one is not necessarily saying that the office and work in varying degrees of clarity did not exist from the beginning of the life of the Church.

The Synod states that the "apostles and community of faithful united with one another by a mutual link under Christ . . . belong to the original inalienable structure of the Church."[15] The initial act of passing on the apostolic power is seen in the transmission of those powers "to their immediate cooperators"[16] so that "the mission assigned to them might continue after their death . . ."[17] Here it seems that the document is saying that those apostolic functions that formed part of the life and work of the apostles were passed on intact, in so far as they could be transmitted, to another generation. The document does not delve into the problem of the gradual manner in which offices came to be named or the way in which powers were located in a specific ministerial order. But it does note that certain powers existed and were transmitted within the Church from the beginning.

The Synod determines that one part of the mission assigned to the apostles and transmitted to their cooperators was "the proclamation of the gospel, the gathering together and leading of the community, by remitting sins, and especially by celebrating the Eucharist."[18] Here we are offered a view of the office of the priest, as a participation in the duties and mission of those who succeeded the apostles. But at no time is a time schedule worked out to indicate when the actual structure of a priestly ministry was fully recognized within the community of believers. Given the overlapping of ministries, Brown places this recognition nearly a century later. This seems to be, in effect, a way of saying that the fuller implications and exclusive nature of the priestly ministry required time to stabilize themselves within the fledgling

Church. This seems all the more reasonable since Brown speaks of the functions as existing from the beginning and of those who did perform them. He reserves his conclusions for the designation of those who relatively rapidly within the life span of the Church came to be named by the exclusive assumption of these functions. The Synod, on the other hand, implies — but does not assert — that the recognition by the community of the specific office of priest was evident from the beginning. However, even in this, the Synod concerns itself with the priestly function, and sees it as existing from the first days of the Church, and as performed by specific ministers.

If the chronology of the matter is put to one side, the question can become one of recognizing what as a function both the Synod and Brown state was a reality from the beginning. The Synod is not offering an exegesis that accounts for a recognition by the community everywhere and all places of the division of ministries and functions. It addresses the study to the existence of sacerdotal powers and an essential hierarchical order of ministries and sees both as belonging "to the original inalienable structure of the Church."[19] Its preoccupation is with the function and its exercise. The problem of its exegetical identification nominally and exclusively is not broached.

Father Brown, in establishing exegetically a chronology for the full development and recognition of the hierarchical structure in the Church, offers a timetable that takes into consideration the gradual awareness by the community of the distinct status of the priesthood and the fuller implications of the Eucharistic sacrifice united to a unique priesthood.

"The priesthood represents the combination or distillation of several distinct roles and special ministries in the NT Church. And in fact some of those other roles and ministries that funneled into the formal priesthood (as it emerged somewhere in the course of the 2nd century) have colored the basic understanding of what a priest should be more than have the task of celebrating the eucharistic sacrifice and the OT background with which that task was associated."[20]

This can also be seen as a statement not of doctrinal variance with the Synod but of a view of the chronological development of the understanding of a reality that required time to be fully appreciated. To say that the office of priesthood was not fully understood in the primitive Church in the same way that it is today, or articulated exactly as it is at the moment, is not to deny that such an order and function existed from the beginning.

The doctrinal statement of the Synod confirms the existence of a priesthood as an essential part of the apostolic Church. Father Brown's study confines itself and its conclusions to an interpretation of how the priesthood gradually came to be seen as one specific office, even though that office was not specifically named in the first years of the Church.

Brown's position from the exegetical point of view does not necessarily find itself at odds with the Synod's position if we consider that the former speaks from strictly exegetical data and premises which seek to see what the first Christian community recognized in the Church as Christ's heritage. The Synod speaks from the magisterial viewpoint of the Church's self-understanding. In such a position she looks to the data of scriptural studies as only one source of her "input," so to speak. Brown, on the other hand, given his stated limited area of study, must confine his conclusions to those supportable directly and immediately by his sole source, Scripture.

If we interpret Father Brown's position as an assertion that the priesthood as we know it today came into existence only later in the history of the Church, then we have the difficulty of seeing in Brown's texts more than seems to be stated. His conclusions seem to be based on an exegesis of the New Testament texts that points to the gradual distillation within the community — or at least within its self-expression in written form — of several functions into one exclusive priesthood. This interpretation of Scripture still affirms the existence from the beginning of certain functions and specific ministries. It leaves open to interpretation the question: How did certain functions come to be localized in specific ministries if they were not recognized as part of that ministry from the beginning? What precisely was the reason for the almost immediate location of so many distinctly sacramental functions within the ministerial priesthood? Was such a development little more than a gradual clarification of concepts and matching titles intuited by the community from the beginning?

The Synod document does not so much tackle the problem of chronology in the development of understanding within the Christian community as it undertakes to state the doctrinal conclusion that the priesthood is an essential hierarchical structure of apostolic origin.[21] In one sense the problem can be seen as one that involves the gradual complete recognition of an exclusive priesthood according to the more precise definition of functions always performed within the Church. This gradual complete recognition does not affirm that the reality did not exist from the beginning. It only implies that in the organization of the primitive Church the fuller recognition or identification of the exclusive nature of the priesthood took time. The reality of an exercised functional priesthood, however, is not denied.

Father Brown considers the Christian priesthood the result of "four principal roles or ministries that ultimately funneled into the Christian priesthood. These ministries are: disciple, the apostle, the presbyter-bishop, and the celebrant of the Eucharist."[22]

Discipleship for Brown is essentially a totally committed witness. He sees it as "almost a monomaniacally consuming vocation, occupying all the interest of the disciple and allowing no competitive diversion whatsoever."[23] One accepted discipleship in order to work within the Christian Community that Jesus might be worthily represented to others.[24] The ministry was a permanent one that resulted from the acceptance of the call to witness Jesus Christ to others in an exemplary manner within the Church and to those still outside her.[25]

The "keynote of apostleship," states Brown, "is service."[26] This service is rendered to Jesus. The apostles serve Christ by representing to others the one in whose name he comes and by "carrying not only the sender's authority but even his presence to others."[27] The exclusiveness of apostleship is found in the fact that one who is an apostle is set apart.[28] When one serves as an apostle he is taken apart from the community — but not out of it — to make the presence of Christ felt in a special way. The apostles speak with authority since they represent Christ. The authority of the apostles extends to the correction of others within the community and the right to speak with authority in matters pertaining to the doctrinal and charitable life of the community.[29]

The apostle, being a missionary figure within the fuller Christian community, moves from one congregation to found still another. In his wake he leaves another to carry on his work. This "other" is in the New Testament the presbyter-bishop. The character trait of the presbyter-bishop, according to Brown, reflects the highly institutional nature of this figue. He must be "above reproach, temperate, sensible, dignified, hospitable, an apt teacher, gentle and not quarrelsome (I Tm 3:1–7; Ti 1:7–9)".[30] His work insures the continuation of the Apostolic ministry and mission.[31]

Finally we come to the ministry of the one who presides at the Eucharist. For him we find no special name. Yet, as Brown notes:

> "The only thing of which we can be reasonably sure is that someone must have presided at the Eucharistic meals and that those who participated acknowledged his right to preside."[32]

We do not know how he got this right to preside.[33] But one most assuredly did perform this sacred function, Brown continues. He also notes that in a short time the right to preside at the Eucharist eventually became the exclusive privilege of bishops and presbyters.[34]

Finally he adds:

> "Subsequently, for a long time most of the reflections about priesthood will be centered on the bishop . . . Until size . . . created a new situation, all that we would consider the normal pastoral and sacramental duties of a priest were exercised regularly by the bishop himself."[35]

From the study of Brown's work we can conclude that in the New Testament there are mentioned various functions within the early Church that were to be carried on indefinitely in the life of the Church. Essentially these functions were: to witness Christ in an exemplary manner; to speak in his name with authority; to insure that the work of the apostles was continued; and to preside at the Eucharist. Brown notes that in the exercise of all these functions the NT does not state precisely where such functions overlapped in the person of any one minister. Nor does the NT state that all these functions, exclusive of the actual ministry of the original apostles, were not found in any one person.

When treating the same subject, the Synod concentrates on the work — the ministry — rather than the actual name given the one who carries out the work in the pages of Sacred Scripture. In this way, it seems, the Synod is more concerned with what was and is to be done rather than who was named or not named with a title while doing the work in the NT.

The parallel between Brown's ministries taken as functions and the Synod's description of the work of a priest is clear. The Synod speaks of the mission and ministry of the witness of the priest. He is a permanent exemplar of the works and the way of life and world view of Jesus. He is an authentic and authoritative representative of Jesus at the service of the Lord in all those works that help the fellowship of the faithful — the Church. The mission of the priest (for the Synod) is that of Christ and is a continuation of the work of the apostles. Finally the Synod notes that the ministry of the priest reaches its summit in the celebration of the Eucharist.

The Synod sees all these functions as part of the ministry of the priest and locates that ministry's origin in apostolic times. Furthermore, it calls that ministry an essential part of the divinely-constituted hierarchy of the Church. In its exegetical section (Part One, section 4) it makes no effort to show the use of *names* within the NT to make its point. It seems rather to teach that the functions and ministries — diverse as they may have been — were seen from the beginning as located in certain members of the community. These people the Church called — if not expressly in the NT, certainly from earliest times — priests. It seems that both agree that certain functions were carried on in the Church from its first days. It also seems that we have no detailed description of who carried on which works — if they were, in fact, performed by diverse groups of the faithful. But the fact remains that certain works were performed. Specific persons performed those actions. The point of difference seems to be centered in the designation of when these functions were located exclusively in the priesthood. The Synod sees the existence of the function and the almost immediate identification by the Christian community of that function as the work of a priest as indication that the formal priesthood existed as is from the beginning. Brown opts for an intervention of several decades or even a century before this formalization took place.

It does not seem to do violence to Brown's work to see the parallels that exist between his study and the document of the Synod. His study is a scriptural one. His object is to see what the NT says explicitly on the function of priests and bishops. Since the texts do not, in textbook fashion, list names and offices, he turns to the functions of which the Scriptures speak. These works as he lists them nearly parallel in an exact manner what the Synod described as the work of the priest today. This is not surprising from a theological point of view. Sacred Scripture exegesis and the expression of the teaching Church should be in accord.

The Synod speaks as a magisterial instrument — however ill-defined the theological "note" of its statements may be. Its work was to point out the essential qualities of the priesthood and to note its primary functions. This it does with a certain reliance on Sacred Scripture. However, that assembly's job was to state the teaching and belief of the Church on the priesthood. In this it needed to consider more than just the words of the New Testament. It considered the Church's appreciation of the acts that Scripture reports. The teaching of the Synod can be seen as the interpretation of works, acts, and functions in the light of the Church's constant understanding of those functions and acts.

Brown offers some valuable insights into expressions found in the NT. Those expressions seem in substance at no point to vary with the Synod's description of a priest. The question of the gradual funneling of diverse functions into one ministry is not answered by the Synod. It speaks only of the functions reported in Sacred Scripture as the functions of a priest. Brown, on the other hand, does not contend that the non-naming of a priest or bishop-presbyter explicitly in the New Testament as the functionary of all the ministries listed there negates the magisterial interpretation of the Church.

The point at issue seems to hang on two points. Brown, as an exegete, faces the question of what exactly does the New Testament say about the ministries of the Christian community. The Synod speaks of the Church's understanding and teaching of those same ministries in the light of the life and expression of the Church's self-understanding. Brown confines his study to a *specifically* defined area. The Synod uses the same New Testament, the object of Brown's study, as only one point — major though it be — in the full expression of its magisterial doctrine.

The underlying premise of any difference between

Brown and the Synod — real or presumed — seems to be the difference in starting points and the necessary limitations imposed by these starting points. Brown is an exegete and is obliged professionally to confine his study to Sacred Scripture and to conclusions directly supportable from his selected texts. The Synod starts from the existential situation and teaches aware of its magisterial prerogatives and duties. It concludes in the light of the Church's understanding of its own Sacred Scripture which itself is a product of the Church's catechetical magisterial mission.

NOTES

1. I, 4.
2. The *Dogmatic Constitution on the Church,* No. 20.
3. I, 4: "Bishops and, on a subordinate level, priests, by virtue of the sacrament of Orders, which confers an anointing of the Holy Spirit and configures to Christ (cf. PO 2), become sharers in the functions of sanctifying, teaching, and governing, and the exercise of these functions is determined more precisely by hierarchical communion (*cf.* LG 24, 27, 28)."
4. *Ibid.*
5. *Ibid.*
6. *Ibid.*
7. *Ibid.*
8. *Ibid.*
9. I, 5.
10. Brown, p. 20.
11. *Ibid.,* p. 13. Cardinal Lawrence Shehan in a recent article echoing a widely made criticism of Brown's theological conclusions seriously questions the very exegesis on which these conclusions are based. Lawrence Cardinal Shehan, "The Priest in the New Testament: Another point of view," *Homilectic & Pastoral Review,* November 1975, pp. 10-23.
12. *Ibid.,* p. 16.
13. *Ibid.,* p. 17: "For the emergence of the idea of a special Christian priesthood in place of the Jewish priesthood several major changes of direction had to intervene. First, Christians had to come to think of themselves as constituting a new religion distinct from Judaism and replacing the Jews of the Synagogue as God's covenated

people. Some Christians may have been (unwittingly?) moving in this direction from a very early period, e.g., the 'left-wing' group called Hellenists in Acts 6:1, if we can judge their theology from the words of Stephen, a Hellenist leader, who attacks the Temple in Acts 7:47–50. But this was scarcely the dominant Christian view before 70."

14. *Ibid.* "This attitude appears in Christian writings about the end of the 1st century or the beginning of the 2nd. *Didache* 14 instructs Christians: 'Assemble on the Lord's Day, breaking bread and celebrating the Eucharist; but first confess your sins that your sacrifice (thysia) may be a pure one . . . For it was of this that the Lord spoke, 'Everywhere and always offer me a pure sacrifice.' The citation is from Mal 1:10, 11, a passage which became a very important factor in the Christian understanding of the Eucharist."

15. I, 4.
16. *Ibid.*
17. *Ibid.*
18. *Ibid.*
19. *Ibid.*
20. Brown, p. 20.
21. In parallel terms we might see the gradual expression of the prerogatives of the See of Peter within the turbulent days of the early Church.
22. *Ibid.*, p. 21.
23. *Ibid.*, p. 22, 23.
24. *Ibid.*, p. 24.
25. *Ibid.*, p. 24, 25.
26. *Ibid.*, p. 27.
27. *Ibid.*, p. 28.
28. *Ibid.*, p. 31.
29. *Ibid.*, p. 32.
30. *Ibid.*, p. 35.
31. *Ibid.*, p. 37.
32. *Ibid.*, p. 41.
33. *Ibid.*
34. *Ibid.*, p. 42.
35. *Ibid.*, p. 43; note 26.

Conclusions

PRIESTLY MINISTRY WAS given to the Church in the mystery of Jesus Christ. It was known from divine revelation. It is understood in the Church. There is no other explanation of "why" or "how" the priesthood. We accept the fact of the priesthood in the context of divine revelation or we have no lasting, authentic foundation for further development. The mystery of priestly ministry is not a question which can be answered by the criteria of human knowledge alone.

The priesthood must be seen in the context of the Church. It is the Church that is primarily responsible for the continuation of Christ's work. It is on this account that its members are called a "priestly people."

All the activity of the Church and its members must be directed to the spread of the Kingdom of God — the completion of Christ's mission.

All the faithful share one faith and one mission. But the participation in the mission is according to degrees of sacramental life and calling. The sacrament of baptism admits one to the Church and enables the believer actively to carry on Christ's work. Baptism joins the believer to Christ and permits him to share in Christ's divine life and mission. But within the Church there is another sacrament that is concerned with the participation in Christ's mission. The sacrament of Orders makes one a sharer in Christ's mission in a special and unique way. By configuring the priest to Christ, the sacrament of Orders makes of the priest an authentic, authoritative and special representative of Christ within the community of believers. As baptism distinguishes the believer from the rest of men by admitting him to the life of Christ, so Orders distinguishes the priest from the rest of the faithful by joining him to Christ in a more full manner. Accordingly, we can say that the mission of Christ is not divided among his followers but that all within his Church participate in it. Some, however, are called to participate more fully. The principle of this differentiation is the sacrament of Orders just as the initial principle of differentiation of the Church from the world is the sacramental life of baptism. By baptism one is made distinct while in the world. By Holy Orders one is made distinct while in the Church.

Since this differentiation is part of the Church as Christ founded it, the hierarchical structure of the Church is by divine plan. The sacred functions that are performed by the priest today are those instituted by Christ and exercised by ministries or Orders established by him in the beginning of the Church's life. The recognition within the Church of the distinct nature of the minister who carried on the sacred activities has always been a part of the Church's self-understanding. However, given the manner of the Church's establishment and first growth, there is no clear nomination within Sacred Scripture of all the offices and functions as one would find in a theology text devoted to the subject. The Synod's statement does not say that all the sacred functions of the priest as we see them today were named as such in the pages of Scripture or that we find there the explicit definition of a priest. Rather it says that specific functions by which Christ was made present to the community were carried out by specific ministers even though the later nominal and theological precisions might not always have been present to the mind of each believer within the Church. A gradual development or clarification of priestly functions does not mean that such functions came into being later in the life of the Church. When we state that the designation by name of a particular office required time, we are not necessarily saying that the office and work do not exist from the beginning of the life of the Church. Rather it seems that those apostolic functions that formed part of the life and work of the apostles were passed on intact to others. For it is agreed that certain powers did exist and were transmitted within the Church from the beginning.

We are led to conclude that the functions of the priest as we know them today existed from the beginning in the Church and the designation of certain believers to perform the sacred functions dates from apostolic times.

The weight of the argument rests on the recognized existence within the first Christian community of specific priestly functions. That some "differentiated" believers performed these functions follows both from the existence of the function — which could not exist without the minister — and the almost immediate identification throughout the whole Church of the function with the priest. The designation of the office of priest by that name may have required several generations to reach universal usage, but the function and the uniqueness of the one who was designated and ordained to perform it was an essential part of the primitive Church. In one sense, the problem can be seen as the gradually complete recognition of an exclusive priesthood. This gradual recognition does not affirm that the reality did not from the beginning exist. It only implies that in the organization of the primitive Church, the fuller recognition or identification of the exclusive nature of the priesthood took time. The reality of an exercised, functional, ministerial priesthood need not be called into question or denied.

In whatever terms the function and its minister were recognized, the sacred action of presenting Christ was seen as the work of selected men. The whole incarnational context of the Church demanded that men be the sharers in the priesthood of Christ as he had been in man's state and condition. Therefore, Christ required specific men to receive and carry on the uniquely fuller powers he wished to leave to his Church. The Synod has an existential, incarnational view of the Church. It sees the Church as that sacrament of Christ and his presence. Holy Orders makes this same presence operative in priests. It seems that this view takes into account the manner of the Church's sacramental existence. It also accounts for the need that Christ through his Church act in a human fashion to reach the believer. The matter boils down to the "how" of the actualization within the

Church of the manifest power to represent Christ. The Synod opts for a concrete actualization and continuity in Holy Orders.

Within the Church, the fullness of the sacrament of Orders is found in the bishop. He is the source and sign of the unity of the Church in faith and charity. He is the principal person whose mission it is to teach and direct the faithful in matters spiritual. Priests share the mission of the bishop because they participate in Sacred Orders. The bishops are to the Church today what the apostles were to the early Church. The Synod holds that the same relationship has been passed on in an unbroken line from the apostles' day to our own and is an essential part of the structure of the Church. Because the bishop cannot reach all those committed in his care, he shares his priestly order with others, thus constituting a subordinate level of Orders.

The apostolic succession then is a reality that is found in individual bishops who trace their powers through the College of Bishops back to the primitive Church. Christ's powers are transmitted through individuals, not just the Church in some conceptual sense. The succession of sacred power in the Church is tied to the Incarnation in its transmission and requires real, living individuals within the Church to be the bearers of Christ's power. The emphasis in this case is not on the historical, cultural, or social influences that colored and formed the style and mood of the expression of priestly office within the Church. By locating the definition of the priesthood in the person of Christ and his works, the Synod prescinds from the historical coloring of the trapping of office. The justification for such an approach theologically is the document's acceptance of the incarnational imperative that any mission need be clothed in the cloth of the day.

Christ's own acceptance of the human condition sets the premise for the Church's incarnational and existential self-evaluation.

The specific work of the person who receives Holy Orders (bishop, priest or deacon) is well explained within the teaching tradition of the Church and defined clearly in both the Council of Trent and Vatican Council II. Priests are ordained in the Church to continue the sacred saving action of Christ which is found in the sacraments. The priest is to gather the faithful for the Eucharistic Sacrifice which he alone can offer in the person and place of Jesus Christ. He is to forgive their sins in the sacrament of penance, again exercising a divine prerogative in the name and person of the Lord. He is to anoint the sick, again utilizing a uniquely priestly power. Among his other specifically priestly functions are: he must pray for the Church, preach the Word, and develop within men the divine life received in baptism by the administration of the other sacraments.

The priest shares in a permanent way the Orders he receives in ordination. The call to priestly duty and service is not a temporary one. It is rooted in the identification of the priest with Christ. As Christ's incarnation required a total giving of self, so the priest's participation in the extension of Christ's mission requires a complete and permanent self-giving. Coupled with the Synod's view of the apostolic succession, the individual permanence of the priesthood confirms the Synod's rejection of a priesthood that is a function to be carried out by temporarily selected member of the community according to the momentary needs of the Church.

Priestly dedication and consecration are found within the context of Christ's authority and work, both of which are permanent. When the priest is ordained, he becomes a manifestation of God's presence and power in this world. This manifestation depends on God and resides in the very essence of the priest. The priest's consecration represents the total self-emptying that was Christ's and also prefigures the day when Christ's Kingdom will reign in fullness. Since the priest is configured to Christ, his priesthood is in some way a permanent part of his being. The priesthood, therefore, is not just for the service of God's people in this stage of the development of the Kingdom, but it is to reflect the permanent and transcendent union of Christ with his Kingdom.

The essential note of the priesthood, which seems to be clear in the Synod's document and made even clearer by a comparison of that document with recent theological reflections, is that a priest by ordination becomes another Christ. Not only his mission but his life is configured to the work and person of Christ. The priest, therefore, participates in Christ's work permanently and efficaciously in and for the whole Church because he is in his very being identified with Christ.

Bibliography

I PRIMARY SOURCES

COUNCIL DOCUMENTS

Acta Synodalia Sacrosancti Concilii Oecumenici Vaticani II. 4 vols. Typis Polyglottis Vaticanis, Vatican City, 1973.

Sacrosanctum Oecumenicum Concilium Vaticanum II. Constitutio Dogmatica De Ecclesia. Sessio V, D. XXI Novembris, MCMLXIV. *Acta Apostolicae Sedis,* LVII, 1. (The Church)

Sacrosanctum Oecumenicum Concilium Vaticanum II. Decretum De Oecumenismo. Session V, D. XXI Novembris, MCMLXIV. *Acta Apostolicae Sedis,* LVII, 90. (Ecumenism)

Sacrosanctum Oecumenicum Concilium Vaticanum II. Decretum De Pastorali Episcoporum Munere in Ecclesia. Sessio VII, D. XXVIII Octobris, MCMLXV. *Acta Apostolicae Sedis,* LVIII, 674. (Bishops' Pastoral Office in the Church)

Sacrosanctum Oecumenicum Concilium Vaticanum II. Decretum De Institutione Sacerdotali. Sessio VII. D. XXVIII Octobris MCMLXV. *Acta Apostolicae Sedis,* LVIII, 713. (Priestly Formation)

Sacrosanctum Oecumenicum Concilium Vaticanum II. Constitutio Dogmatica De Divina Revelatione. Sessio VIII, XVIII Novembris, MCMLXV. *Acta Apostolicae Sedis,* LVIII, 817. (Revelation)

Sacrosanctum Oecumenicum Concilium Vaticanum II. Decretum De Apostolatu Laicorum. Sessio, VIII, D. XVIII Novembris, MCMLXV. *Acta Apostolicae Sedis,* LVIII, 837. (Laity)

Sacrosanctum Oecumenicum Concilium Vaticanum II. Decretum De Activitate Missionali Ecclesiae. Sessio IX, D. VII Decembris, MCMLXV. *Acta Apostolicae Sedis,* LVIII, 947. (Missions)

Sacrosanctum Oecumenicum Concilium Vaticanum II. Constitutio Pastoralis De Ecclesia In Mundo Huius Temporis. Sessio IX, D. VII Decembris, MCMLXV. *Acta Apostolicae Sedis,* LVIII, 1026. (The Church Today)

Sacrosanctum Oecumenicum Concilium Vaticanum III. Decretum De Presbyterorum Ministerio Et Vita. Sessio IX, D. VII Decembris, MCMLXV. *Acta Apostolicae Sedis,* LVIII, 991. (Ministry and Life of Priests)

PAPAL DOCUMENTS

"Acta Pauli Pp. VI: Concilium Oecumenicum Vaticanum II", *Acta Apostolicae Sedis,* LV, 841.

"Acta Pauli Pp. VI: Habita in patriarchali Basilica Vaticana, Eucharistico Sacrificio a Beatissimo Patri concelebrato, ut Episcoporum Synodi coetus inaugurarentur", *Acta Apostolicae Sedis,* LIX, 963.

———, "E. mis Purpuratis Patribus et Exc. mis Praesulibus e Synodo Episcoporum, primo coacto coetui operam navantibus", *Acta Apostolicae Sedis,* LIX, 969.

..........., "Eucharistico Sacrificio peracto, Revmus P. D. Hamletus Tondini, ab Epistulis ad Principes, Summi Pontificis iussu hanc legit Allocutionem, quam Beatissimus Pater peculiari modo ad Exemos Praesules, qui primo Consessui Synodi Episocoporum interfuerunt, directam voluit, cum Coetus ille finem haberet:", *Acta Apostolicae Sedis,* LIX, 1023.

"Commentarium Officiale, "Ad E. mos Patres Cardinales, ad Romanae Curiae Pontificalisque Domus Praelatos, per E. mum Sacri Collegii Decanum Summo Pontifici felicia ac fausta ominatos, Nativitatis Domini nostri Iesu Christi festo recurrente." *Acta Apostolicae Sedis,* XVI, 34.

———, "In Aede Sixtina habita a Beatissimo Patre Sacrum concelebrante, ineunte Extraordinaria Episcoporum Synodo." *Acta Apostolicae Sedis,* XVI, 716.

"Acta Pauli Pp. VI: Habita in Basilica Liberiana, cum coetus haberentur Extraordinariae Episcoporum coactae Synodi", *Acta Apostolicae Sedis,* XVI, 723.

"Commentarium Officiale: E. mis Patribus Cardinalibus et Exc. mis Praesulibus e Synodo Episcoporum, laboribus iam ad finem vergentibus", *Acta Apostolicae Sedis,* XVI, 726.

"Acta Pauli Pp. VI: E. mis Patribus et Exc. mis Praesulibus e Consilio Secretariae Generalis Synodi Episcoporum, qui coetui Romae habito interfuerunt", *Acta Apostolicae Sedis,* LXIII, 133.

L

———, "Ad Benedictinos monachos, in Sublacensi sacro Specu, quo Summus Pontifex, proximo iam die Episcopalis Synodi ineundae, peregrinatus est", *Acta Apostolicae Sedis,* LXIII, 745.

"Commentarium Officiale: In Aede Sixtina habita, Beatissimo Patre Sacrum celebrante, secundo ineunte ordinario Coetu Episcoporum Synodi", *Acta Apostolicae Sedis,* LXIII, 770.

"Acta Pauli Pp. VI: E. mis Patribus Cardinalibus et Exc. mis Praesulibus cum prima haberetur congregatio secundi ordinarii Coetus Synodi Episcoporum", *Acta Apostolicae Sedis,* LXIII, 773.

———, "In Vaticana Basilica Christifidelibus coram admissis", *Acta Apostolicae Sedis,* LXIII, 815.

———, "E. mis Patribus Cardinalibus et Exc. mis Praesulibus e

Synodo Episcoporum, cum secundus ordinarius Coetus exitum haberet", *Acta Apostolicae Sedis,* LXIII, 831.

"Litterae Apostolicae Motu Proprio Datae: Quibus Synodus Episcoporum Pro Universa Ecclesia Constituitur", *Acta Apostolicae Sedis,* LVII, (October 1965), 775-780.

"Litterae Encyclicae: Ad Episcopos, Sacerdotes et Christifedeles totius Catholici Orbis: de sacerdotali Caelibatu", *Acta Apostolicae Sedis,* LIX (August 1967), 657-697.

SYNODAL DOCUMENTS

Synodus Episcoporum, "De Sacerdotio Ministeriali", Typis Polyglottis Vaticanis, MCMLXXI, *Acta Apostolicae Sedis,* LXIII, 898.

Synodus Episcoporum, "De Sacerdotio Ministeriali Lineamenta Argumentorum De Quibus Disceptabitur In Secondo Coetu Generali", Typis Polyglottis Vaticanis, Vatican City, MCMLXXI.

Synodus Episcoporum, "De Sacerdotio Ministeriali Relatio De Parte Doctrinali", Typis Polyglottis Vaticanis, MCMLXXI.

Synodus Episcoporum, "De Sacerdotio Ministeriali Relatio Post Disceptationem Ab Em. mo D. Joseph Card. Höffner, Archiepiscopo Coloniensi Relatore, Proposta Ad Animadversiones A Patribus Synodi Prolatas De Parte Doctrinali", Typis Polyglottis Vaticanis, MCMLXXI.

Synodus Episcoporum, "Exitus Suffragationis Cum Expensione Modorum Super Quinque Propositiones De Sacerdotio Ministeriali", Typis Polyglottis Vaticanis, MCMLXXI.

Synodus Episcoporum, "De Sacerdotio Ministeriali Relatio De Quaestionibus Practicis", Typis Polyglottis Vaticanis, MCMLXXI.

Synodus Episcoporum, "De Sacerdotium Ministeriali Relatio Post Disceptationem Ab Em. mo Vincentio Card. Enrique Y Tarancon Archiepiscopo Toletano, Relatore, Proposta Ad Animadversiones A Patribus Synodi Prolatas De Parte Practica", Typis Polyglottis Vaticanis, MCMLXXI.

Synodus Episcoporum, "Suffragatio Circa Argumentum De Sacer dotio Ministeriali", Typis Polyglottis Vaticanis, MCMLXXI.

"Acta Consilii Pro Publicis Ecclesiae Negotiis", *Acta Apostolicae Sedis,* LXIII, 702.

———, *Acta Apostolicae Sedis,* XVI, 525.

UNPUBLISHED MATERIAL: INTERVENTIONS

All the individual interventions of the Synod on the Ministerial Priesthood. This includes the remarks of each synodal Father for the entire 1971 meeting as presented in the form of an intervention. These can be found in Donald W. Wuerl, "The Priesthood, The Doctrine of the Third Synod of Bishops and recent Theological Conclusions", Extract, Doctoral Dissertation, Angelicum University, Rome, 1974.

"Reports" of the twelve language groups, 8 October 1971.

1. Archbishop Joseph CORDEIRO, of Karachi, Pakistan; reporter for English Language Group A.
2. Rev. Edward L. HESTON, C.S.C., President of the Pontifical Commission for Social Communications; reporter, English Language Group B.
3. Rev. Theodore VAN ASTEN, Superior General of the White Fathers; reporter for English Language Group C.
4. Archbishop Roger ETCHEGARAY, Marseilles, France; reporter for French Language Group A.
5. Rev. Joseph LECUYER, Superior General of the Congregation of the Holy Ghost; reporter for French Language Group B.
6. Bishop Paul Joseph SCHMITT, of Metz, France; reporter, French Language Group C.
7. Bishop Franz HENGSBACH, of Hessen, Germany; reporter, German Language Group.
8. Bishop Octavio Nicolas DERISI, Auxiliary of La Plata, Argentina; reporter, Spanish-Portuguese Group A.
9. Archbishop Marcus McGRATH, of Panama; reporter for Spanish-Portuguese Language Group B.
10. Bishop Juan TORRES OLIVER, of Ponce, Puerto Rico; reporter for Spanish-Portuguese Language Group C.
11. Archbishop Enrico BARTOLETTI, Apostolic Administrator, Lucca, Italy; reporter Italian language Group.
12. S. B. IGNACE PIERRE XVI BATANIAN, of Cilicia of the Armenians; reporter for Latin Language Group.

"Reports" of the language groups, 19 October 1971.

1. Archbishop Joseph CORDEIRO, of Karachi, Pakistan; reporter for English Language Group A.
2. Rev. Edward L. HESTON, C. S. C., President of the Pontificial Commission for Social Communications; reporter, English Language Group B.
3. Rev. Theodore VAN ASTEN, Superior General of the Missionaries of Africa; reporter for English Language Group C.
4. Archbishop Roger ETCHEGARAY, Marseilles, France; reporter for French Language Group A.
5. Rev. Joseph LECUYER, Superior General of the Congregation of the Holy Ghost; reporter for French Language Group B.
6. Bishop Paul Joseph SCHMITT, of Metz, France; reporter, French Language Group C.
7. Bishop Franz HENGSBACH, of Hessen, Germany; reporter, German Language Group.
8. Bishop Octavio Nicolas DERISI, Auxiliary of La Plata, Argentina; reporter, Spanish-Portuguese Group A.

9. Archbishop Marcus McGRATH, of Panama; reporter for Spanish-Portuguese Language Group B.
10. Bishop Juan TORRES OLIVER, of Ponce, Puerto Rico; reporter for Spanish-Portuguese Language Group C.

Synodus Episcoporum, "Parte Dogmatica Analisi delle risposte prevenute dalle conferenze Episcopali", Preparatory material processed as the result of the interventions sent to the Synod Office and prepared as the basis of the document "De Sacerdotio Ministeriali Relation De Parte Doctrinali".
Consisting of reports from the Episcopal Conferences as they are listed in the original Analysis:

AFRICA:
Madagascar
Rodesia
Senegal
Tanzania

AMERICA LATINA:
Porto Rico
Costa Rica
Paraguay

AMERICA SETTENTRIONALE:
Canada
Stati Uniti

ASIA:
Giappone
Iraq
Corea

EUROPA:
Belgio
Germania
Italia
Polonia
Portogallo
Scozia
Cecoslovacchia

OCEANIA:
Australia
Nuova Zelanda

CURIAL DOCUMENTS

"Sacra Congregatio Pro Clericis Litterae Circulares ad Praesides Conferentiarum Episcopalium de Consiliis Presbyteralibus iuxta placita Congregationis Plenariae die 10 Octobris 1969 habitae", Acta Apostolicae Sedis, LXII (February 1970) 123-134.

"Sacra Congregatio Pro Clericis Litterae Circulares Ad Patriarchas, Primates, Archiepiscopos, Episcopos Aliosque Locorum Ordinarios De Conciliis Pastoralibus Iuxta Placita Congregationis Plenariae Mixtae Die 15 Martii 1972 Habitae", (Unpublished).
"Sacra Congregation Pro Doctrina Fidei Declaratio circa catholicam doctrinam de Eccelsia contra nonnullos errores hodiernos tuendam", *L'Osservatore Romano,* Anno CXIII, N. 152, 34, 833.

EPISCOPAL DOCUMENTS

ANTILLES:

Antilles Episcopal Conference, "The Ministerial Priesthood", Kingston (Jamaica), June 1971.

BRAZIL:

Conferencia Nacional dos Bispos do Brasil, "Sacerdocio Ministeriale", Petropolis, June 1971.

———, Secretariat, "Report", Church, Structures and Diversification in the Ministry, S. N. A. M. H. I., Itaici, 1970.

CANADA:

Canadian Catholic Conference, Committee of Bishops and Priests, "A Working Paper on the Ministerial Priesthood in Preparation for Synod 1971", Ottawa, July 1971.

CELAM:

Consejo Episcopal Latin America: "Indigenas mexicanos hablan del sacerdocio; Indigenas del Ecuador comentan sobre sacerdocio", San Jose (Costa Rica), XIII Reunion Ordinaria del CELAM, May 1971.

———, "Resultado de grupos regionales sobre 'Sacerdocio' ".

GERMANY:

Deutschen Bischofskonferenz: "De Ministerio Sacerdotali", Munich, September 1971.

———, "Priesterbriefe zur Arbeitsgrundlage der Bischofssynode uber 'Das priesterliche Dienstamt' ", Munich, August 1971.

———, "Weitere Ergebnisse der Priesterumfrage", Sekretariat der Deutschen Bischofskonferenz, July 1971.

HOLLAND:

Nederlandse Bisschoppen-Konferentie, "Bemerkingen bij het Synodedokument 'De sacerdotio ministeriali' ", Tilburg, July 25, 1971.

INDIA:

Catholic Bishops Conference of India, "Memorandum on the Subject of the Ministerial Priesthood; General Remarks on the Synod Text". New Delhi, August 1971.

ITALY:

Conferenza Episcopale Italiana, "Fondamenti Biblico-Teologici Del

Sacerdozio Ministeriali", VI Assemblea Generale, Roma, 6-11 Aprile 1971.

MEXICO:

Reunion Interamericana de Obispos: "La porblematica sacerdotal en nuestro continente", Mexico City, May 18-21, 1971.

PERU:

Conferencia Episcopal del Peru, Comision Episcopal del Clero, "Sobre el Sacerdocio Ministerial", Lima, August 1971.

———, "Documento de la Comision Episcopal del Clero en preparacion al Sinodo", Lima, July 19, 1971.

SCANDANAVIA:

Conferentia Episcopalis Scandiae, "Uddrag af den nordiske bispekonference", Stockholm, July 21, 1971.

U.S.A.:

United States Catholic Conference, "Documentation for General Meeting of National Conference of Catholic Bishops, Detroit, Michigan, 27-29 April; Report of Ad Hoc Bishops' Committee on Priestly Life and Ministry", Washington, April 1971.

II SECONDARY SOURCES

I. Offical Press Releases of the Vatican Press Office for the Synod.

Synodus Episcoporum, Comitato per l'Informazione, Vatican City September 30, 1971 — November 6, 1971.

II. IDOC Series of Documents and Studies on the Synod.

International Documentation of the Contemporary Church (IDOC) Rome, 1971; SS71-1 Remarks Concerning the Synod Document "De Sacerdotio Ministeriali".

———, SS-71-2. "The Priestly Ministry"

———, SS71-3. "National Federation of Priests' Councils Statements".

———, SS71-6. "Commentaries et Suggestions de l'Eglise Canadienne concernant le projet de schema synodal sur le Sacerdoce Ministeriel".

———, SS71-19. "Le Grand Combat de l'Eglise Latine pour le Celibat des Clercs".

———, SS71-21. "Human Growth in the Priesthood".

———, SS71-32. "Recontre Europeenne des Delegues des Conseils Presbyteraux".

———, SS71-55. "Analysis of the Interventions on Celibacy".

III OTHER WORKS CONSULTED

"After the Synod", *America,* Vol. 125, No. 16, November 20, 1971.

Aquinas, St. Thomas, *Summa Theologica,* Vols. 3, Benziger, New York, 1948.

———, *Opera Omnia,* Typographia Polyglotta, Rome, 1888.

Alcala, Manuel, "Retrospectiva critica del Sinodo Episcopal", *Razon y Fe,* 1971, pp. 473-482.

Alessandrini, Federico, "Il Sinodo", *L'Osservatore della domenica,* November 14, 1971.

Alfrink, Bernard Jan. Card., "Crisis in the Priesthood", *Tablet,* 223, 1969, p. 1056.

Allmen, J. J. von, "L'Eglise locale parmi les autres Eglises locales", *Irénikon,* 43, 1970, pp. 512-537.

Ambrosianio, A., "Sacerdozio ministeriale ed Eucaristia", *Asprenas,* 17, 1970.

Ancel, Alfred, Ev., "Insertion du pretre dans le monde", *Seminarium,* 9, 1969, pp. 114-134.

Ashton, John, "The Document on the Priesthood", *Month,* Vol. CCXXXII, Vol. CCXXXXI, Vol. 1250, October 1971.

Aumann, Jordan, "Editorial: The Priest and Church Renewal", *Priest,* 25, 1969, pp. 514-516.

Aumont, Michele, "Elements bibliographiques", *Le Pretre, homme du sacré,* 2e ed., Desclée, Paris, 1969.

Bacqué, Francois, "Les Conférences épiscopales ont renoué avec la tradition la plus authentique de l'Eglise", *L'Osservatore Roma no',* 1014, 1969.

Baker, Kenneth, "A Report on the Synod Reporting", *Homiletic and Pastoral Review,* Vol. LXXII, No. 8, May, 1972.

———, "A milestone for collegiality: the third Synod of bishops", *Homiletic and Pastoral Review,* January 1972.

Barker, Glenn W., Lane, William L. (and) Michaels, J. Ramsey, "First Peter: A Royal Priesthood", *The New Testament Speaks,* Harper and Row, New York, 1969.

Bartoletti, Enrico, "Il prete dopo il Sinodo". *Città Nuova,* November 25, 1971.

———, "Problemi del sacerdozio ministeriale", *Coscienza,* November 1971.

Becker, K. J., *Der priesterliche Dienst, II, Wesen und Vollmachten des Priesterlums nach dem Lehramt.* (Quaestiones disputatae, 47) Herder, Freiburg-Basel-Wien, 1970.

Begley, John, "The Office and Ministry of Priests", *American Ecclesiastical Review,* Vol. CLXV, No. 2, October 1971.

Beni, Arialdo, "Il sacerdozio ministeriale al Sinodo dei vescovi", *La Rivista del clero italiano,* 1972.

Berquist, Millard J. (et al) "Personal Perspectives (on Ordination)", *Southwestern Journal of Theology,* 11, Spring 1969.

Bertrams, W., S. I., "De differentia inter sacerdotium episcoporum et presbyterorum", *Periodica de re Mor. Can. Lit.*, 59, 1970.

Betti, Umberto, "Sinodo e sacerdozio", *L'Osservatore Romano,* January 12, 1972.

Bieder, W. "Die Reichsgestalt der Kirche nach dem Neuen Testament", *Kirchenblatt fur die Reformierte Schweiz,* 125, 1969, pp. 130-133.

Bifet, Juan Esquerda, "El Sinodo no es la unica ni la principal manera de expresar la colegialidad episcopal", *Ecclesia,* May 6, 1972.

Blake, Richard A., "Facing a New Priesthood", *Catholic World,* 209, 1969.

Blanc, Ed. "Réflexions sur la crise actuelle de l'Eglise", *Economie et Humanisme,* 188, 1969.

Blank, J., "Kirchliches Amt und Priesterbegriff", *Zeltpriester nach dem Konzil,* Kosel-Verleg, Munchen, 1969.

Blazquez, Feliciano, "El II Sinodo general de Obispos", *Heches y Dichos,* August-September, 1971.

Bonati, Milena, "Il prete è un centro storico. Intervista con P. Balducci", *Politica,* 21, November 1971.

Bonicelli, Gaetano, "Sacerdozio ministeriale e giustizia nel mondo", *Orientamenti pastorali,* 1971.

Bortolotti, Roberto, "La Disciplina giuridica dei rapporti delle conferenze episcopali nazionali con la Sede Apostolica e delle conference stesse tra di lore", *Civiltà Cattolica* 120, III, 1969.

Bovo, Luigi, "Il Sinodo dei vescovi: l'esodo dei preti", *Rocca,* October 15, 1971.

———, "I problemi tornano alla communità, *Rocca,* November 15, 1971.

Boulgakov, S., "L'Eglise comme organisation sacramentelle et hiérarchique", *Messager Orthodoxe,* 46-47, 1969, pp. 21-44.

Bourdeau, F., "Pouvoir et autorité dans l'Eglise", *Dossiers de l'Union,* 1, 1969.

Bourke, M. M., "The Catholic Priest: Man of God for Others", *Worship,* 43, 1969.

Bouyer, L., *L'Eglise de Dieu. Corps du Christ et temple de l'Esprit,* Ed du Cerf, Paris, 1970.

Brechet, Raymond, "La fin du clergé, *Choisir,* November 1971.

———, "A l'aube d'un jour nouveau", *Choisir,* December 1971.

Brown, Raymond, *Priest and Bishop: Biblical Reflections,* Paulist Press, New York, 1970.

———, *The Gospel According to St. John.* two vols., Chapman, London, 1971.

———, "The Changing Face of the Priesthood", *America,* May 20, 1972.

Bunnik, Ruud J., *Priests for Tomorrow,* Holt, Rinehart and Winston, New York, 1969.

———, *Pretres des temps nouveaux,* Casterman, Paris, 1969.

Burgalassi, Silvano, *Preti in Crisi?,* Esperienze, Fossano, 1970.

Bussi, N., "La problematica teologica attuale attorno al ministero sacerdotale", *Presenza Pastorale,* 1970.

Burtness, James H., "Ministry and Ordination", *Dialog,* 8, 1969.

Calkins, A. B., "John Henry Newman on Conscience and the Magisterium", *Downside Review,* 1969, pp. 358-369.

Campion, Donald R., "Synod Notebook", *America,* 125, 1971, pp. 253, 278, 308, 338, 364, 391, 418-419.

Capmany, J., "Los teologos y el magisterio de la Iglesia en el movimento pastoral del postconcilio", *Teol. Espir.,* 13, 1969.

Cappanera, Raoul, "Le malaise sacerdotal, à partir de revues", *Masses Ouvrières,* 263, 1969.

Caprile, Giovanni, "Il Sacerdote oggi", *Civiltà Cattolica,* 120, I, 1969.

———, "Il Sinodo dei Vescovi", *La Civiltà Cattolica,* Ann. 122, Vol. 4, 1971.

———, "Il Terzo Sinodo dei vescovi", Cronache, *Civiltà Cattolica,* 1971, I, pp. 280-284; IV, pp. 161-165; 262-271; 366-386; 472-493.

———, *Il Sinodo dei Vescovi 1971,* Edizioni "La Civiltà Cattolica", 2 vols. Rome, 1972.

———, "Le Synode de 1971", *Nouvelle Revue Théologique,* 1972.

———, "I religiosi alla seconda assemblea generale del Sinodo dei vescovi", *Vita consacrata,* 1972.

Caprioli, Venanzio, "In margine al decreto del Sinodo 'Il sacerdozio ministeriale'," *Rivista di vita spirituale,* 1972.

Cardinale, H. E., "The Episcopal Ministry", *One in Christ,* 5, 1969.

Carli, L. M., "Competenze e modo di procedere delle Conferenze episcopali nazionali", *Palestra del Clero,* 48, 1969, pp. 8-23.

———, *Le Conferenze episcopal nazionali,* Istituto Padano di Arti Grafiche, Rovigo, 1969.

Carr, Aidan M., "Contest: the Priest of the 70's; editorial", *Homiletic and Pastoral Review,* 69, 1968-69.

Carroll, Thomas P., "The N.F.P.C. Convention vs. The Priest's Identity Crisis", *Homiletic and Pastoral Review,* 69, 1968-69.

Casanova, Antoine, "Du Concile au Synode", *Vatican II et l'evolution de l'Eglise,* Ed. Sociales, Paris, 1969.

Casey, Leo J., "The Priest of the '70's; Western Canadian Conference", *Homiletic and Pastoral Review,* 69, 1968-69.

Castillo, Josè M., Sinodo 1971, "Cara y cruz", *Estudios Eclesiasticos,* 1972.

"Catalogue of Documents Synod of Bishops Supplement N. 1", *IDOC,* Rome, October 1971.
Catta, Etienne, "Lettre aux membres du Synode", *La Pensee Catholique,* 1971.
Centro Dehoniano, ed., *Enchiridion Vaticanum,* Bologna, 1970.
Charalambidis, S., Lagny, G., Granger, E., Schaller, R., *Le diaconat,* Ed. Mame, Paris, 1970.
"Che Cosa Dobbiam Attenderci", *La Civiltà Cattolica,* Ann. 122, Vol. 4, 1971.
Chenevert, Jacques, "Le Synode . . . et après?", *Relations,* November 1971.
Christian priesthood, ed. N. Lash, J. Rhymer, Longman and Todd, London, 1970.
"The Church", *Irish Theological Review,* Vol. 36, 1969.
The Church in Our Day, United States Conference of Catholic Bishops, Washington, D.C., 1966.
Cipriani, Settimio, "A proposito del libro 'La Chiesa' di Hans Küng", *Asprenas,* 16, 1969.
———, "La dottrina del sacerdozio nel Nuovo Testamento", *Asprenas,* 17, 1970.
Cleary, William H., ed., *Hyphenated Priests; the ministry of the future,* Corpus Publi., Washington, 1969.
Clifford, Dermot, "The Image of the Bishop", *Furrows,* Vol. 22, No. 8, August 1971.
Cody, Aelred, "Bibliography", *A History of Old Testament Priesthood,* Pontifical Biblical Institute, Rome, 1969, pp. xvi-xxvii.
Collela, P., De Petris, P., "Note sul III Sinodo dei vescovi", *Il Tetto,* 1971.
Colella, Pasquale, "Brevi osservazioni sul Sinodo des Vescovi", *Diritto Ecclesiastico,* 80, I, 1969.
"Collegiality in Practice", *Herder Correspondence,* 6, 1969.
Colombo, Arrigo, "Per un rinnovamento dell'istituto sinodale", *Il Regno Attualità,* 1972.
Concetti, Gino, *Bilancio e Documenti dei Vescovi,* Massimo, Milan, 1968.
———, "Priests and Vatican II", *L'Osservatore Romano* (English), 53, 1969.
———, "Il sacerdozio presbiteriale", *Mondo Cattolico,* Nov.-Dec. 1971.
Congar, Yves-Marie-Joseph, *Au milieu des orages; l'Eglise affronte aujourd'hui son avenir,* Ed. du Cerf, Paris, 1969.
———, *Esquisses du Mystere de l'Eglise,* Cerf, Chartes, 1965.
———, *Le Christ, L'Unique Pretre, et Nous ses Pretres,* Alsatia, Paris, 1965.

———, *The Mystery of the Church,* Chapman, London, 1965.
———, *The Pentecost,* Cerf, Chartes, 1965.
———, *Una Chiesa contestata,* Queriniana, Brescia, 1969.
———, "Bulletin d'ecclesiologie (1): L'Eglise de Hans Küng", *Revue des Sciences Philosophiques et Theologiques,* 53, 1969.
———, "Eclaircissements sur la question des ministères", *La Maison Dieu,* 1970.
———, "Le problème ecclésiologique de la papauté après Vatican II", *Intern. Kirchl. Zeitschr.,* 60, 1970.
———, *Ministeres et Communion Ecclesiale,* Paris, 1971.
———, "Remarks about the Documentary work on the priestly ministry proposed in view of the Synod of Bishops", Le Saulcoir, Paris, 1971.
———, "Nouvelle Revue Theologique", No. 8, October 1972.
Contreras, Navia, "Pautos para el estudio del documento del Sinodo acerca del sacerdocio", August 10, 1972; ciclostilato.
Cooper, Joel, "Ordained to Word, Sacrament and Order", *Duke Divinity School Review,* 34, Winter 1969.
Coppens, J., "L'Eglise dans l'optique de Hans Küng", *Ephem, Theol. Lov.,* 46, 1970.
———, "Le sacerdoce chrétien, II. Des Pères apostoliques a Vatican II", *Nouv. Rev. Théol.,* 92, 1970.
———, *Sacerdoce et Celibat Etude Historique,* Duculot, Gembloux, 1971.
Cothenet, E., "Le Problème de l'Eglise, d'après l'ouvrage de Hans Küng", *Esprit et vie,* 79, 1969.
Cowdrey, H.E.J., "The Dissemination of St. Augustine's Doctrine of Holy Orders during the Later Patristic Age", *Journal of Theological Studies,* 20, 1969.
"Crisis in the Church: a hard look at where we were and, hopefully, where we are going in the years ahead", *Commonweal,* 91, 1969-70.
Cusson, Gilles, "On demande des gourous", *Relations,* November 1971.
Dagras, Michel, "Sacerdoce et service de la communauté des chrétiens", *Pretres Diocésains,* 107, 1969, pp. 7-13.
Dalla Torre, Giuseppe, Jr., "Il Sinodo ha rafforzato la collegialità", *Studi Cattolici,* 1971.
Danielou, Jean Card., "Crisis in the Church", *L'Osservatore Romano* (English), 85, 1969, p. 8.
———, "Origins of the Ministerial Priesthood", *L'Osservatore Romano* (English), 8(152), February 25, 1971.
———, "La signification du Synode", *La Nouvelle Revue des deux Mondes,* 1972.

del Portillo, Alvaro, "L'immagine del sacerdote", *Studi Cattolici,* 1972.

De Giorgis E., "Un Sinodo per chi e per che cosa?", *Vita Sociale,* 1971.

Delhaye, Philippe, "Le troisième Synode épiscopale et le problème des pretres", *Esprit et vie,* 1972, pp. 65-70; 97-108; 161-168; 177-188.

Dejaifve, Georges, "Vatican II et le Synode épiscopal", *Nouvelle Revue Théologique,* 91, 1969.

De Letter, P., "Episcopal Conferences", *The Clergy Monthly,* 33, 1969.

———, "The Synod of Bishops 1971", *The Clergy Monthly,* 1972.

———, "Interview: The Priesthood according to Scripture and Tradition", France Catholique, No. 1295, October 8, 1971.

DeRosa, Giuseppe, "Il documento sinodale sul sacerdozio", *Civiltà Cattolica,* 1972, I, pp. 226-237; 343-357; 439-453; II, pp. 21-36.

de Vaucelles, Louis, "Journal du Synode", *Etudes,* December 1972.

———, "Reflexions post-synodales", *Etudes,* January 1972.

Dhanis, Tony, "Le Synode, un echec?", *La Foi et le Temps,* December 1971.

Digan, Parig, "The Four Futures of the Priesthood", *Furrows,* Vol. 22, No. 9, September 1971.

Dillenschnedier, C., Il *Sacerdozio Nostro Nel Sacerdozio di Cristo,* Dehoniane, Bologna, 1966.

Di Monda, Antonio M., "Il Sinodo dei vescovi nel mondo di oggi", *Palestra del clero,* 1971.

"Doctrinal Debates", *Herder Correspondence,* Vol. 6, No. 12, December 1969.

"Documentary Service", United States Catholic Conference, Washington, D.C., April 29, 1971.

Dombois, Hans, "The Basic Structure of Church Law", *Concilium* (American), 48, 1969.

Dominian, J., "The Available Priesthood; the sacred ministry", *Theology,* 72, 1969.

Döpfner, Julius Card., "Das Bleibende und Sich-Wandelnde im Priestertum der Kirche", *Schweizerische Kirchenzeitung,* 137, 1969.

"Dossier sul Sinodo: Chi fa piangere il Papa", *L'Europeo,* 25 November 1971.

Dubois, Marcel, "Le Role du célébrant et des ministres du culte", *Documentation Liturgique,* 12, 1969.

Ducos, M., O. P., *Des pretres parlent du fonctionnement de l'Eglise,* Ed. Fleurus, Paris, 1970.

Dulles, Avery, "Ecclesiological Opinions", *Month,* Vol. CCXXXII, No. 1251, November 1971.

———, "Summary of the Paper for the Fourth International Meeting of Jesuit Ecumenists held in Dublin, August 1971", *Month,* Vol. CCXXXII, No.1251, November 1971.

———, "The Contemporary Magisterium", *Theology Digest,* 17, 1969.

Echlin, Edward P., "The Once and Future Priesthood", *Review for Religious,* 28, 1969.

Edwards, A., "Existencia sacerdotal?", *Sal Terrae,* 57, 1969.

Ellis, John Tracy, "Our gifts differ", *Future Forms of Ministry,* Mundelein, Illinois, 1971.

Enrique y Tarancon, Vicente Card., "Caminos para la solucion de los problemas actuales del Clero", *Incunable,* 240, 1969.

Espeja, J., O.P., "Ministro de la comumidad sacerdotal. Para teologia del presbiterado en el Vaticano II., *Teologia del Sacerdocio ministerial y laical,* Ed. Aldecoa, Burgos, 1970.

Esquerda, Bifet, J., "La teologia del sacerdocio en revision", *Seminarium,* 1969.

———, "Boletin bibliografico de teologia sobre el sacerdocio (1968-1969)", *Teologia del sacerdocio. Sacerdocio ministerial y laical,* Ed. Aldecoa, Burgos, 1970.

Every, George, "Sacralisation et secularisation en Orient et en Occident durant le premier millenaire apres le Christ", *Concilium,* (Français), 47, 1969.

Fabro, Nando, "Il terzo Sinodo dei vescovi", Il Gallo, November 1971.

Fabro, Nando, Pavan, Adalberto, "Il terzo Sinodo dei vescovi", Il Gallo, January 1972.

Fagan, S., "What's Happening to Priests?", *Doctrine and Life,* 1969.

Fagiolo, V, Concetti, Gino, Ed. *La Collegialità episcopale per il futuro della Chiesa,* Vallecchi, Firenze, 1969.

Fahrnberger, G. *Bischofsant und Priestertum in den Diskussionen des Konzils von Trent Eine rechtstheologische Untersuchung* (Wiener Beitrage fur Theologie, Bd. XXX) Herder, Wien, 1970.

Farhat, Edmond, "La II assemblée generale du Synode des eveques 1971," "Monitor Ecclesiasticus 1972."

Favale, A.; Gozzelino G., "Il ministero presbiterale. Fenomenologia e diagnosi di una crisi; dottrina; spiritualità," *Testo del Documento De sacerdotio ministeriali del Sinodo dei Vescovi 1971,* Elle Di Ci, Leumann, Turin, 1972.

———, "De Sacerdotio Ministeriali del Sinodo dei Vescovi 1971," Leumann, Turin, 1972.

Fernandez, A., "El Sinodo de los obispos y la colagialidad episcopal," *Scripta Theologica,* 1969.
———, "La diferencia entre el sacerdocio comun de los fieles y el sacerdocio ministerial en los debates concillares del Vaticano II," *Scripta Theologica,* 1969.
Ferrara, Vincenzo, "Il Sinodo dei Vescovi tra ipotesi e realtà; natura teologico — giuridica del Sinodo dei Vescovi nel Magistero di Paolo VI e nella dottrina conciliare," *Apollinari 42,* 1969.
Fesquet, Henri, *Le Synodode et l'avenir de l'Eglise,* Ed. du Centurion, Paris, 1972.
Filippi, Alfio, "Dalla crisi del prete alla crisi del Sinodo," *Il Regno Attualità,* 1972.
Fourez, Gerard, "The Priesthood in Modern Society", *Chicago Studies 8,* 1969.
Fransen, Piet, "Orders and Ordination", *Sacramentum Mundi; an encyclopedia of theology,* Palm. Publ., Montreal, 1969.
Fries, Heinrich, *Faith Under Challenge,* Herder, New York, 1969.
Galot, J., "Nouvelle Revue Theologique", No. 9, November 1971.
Galvin, A., "Priests of the New Horizon", *Worldmission,* 20, No. 3, 1969.
Garrigues, J.M., "Le Caractere sacerdotal dans la tradition des Peres grees", *Nouvelle Revue Theologique,* Vol. 108, No. 8, October 1971.
Gherardini, Brunero, *La Chiesa Arca dell'Alleanza,* Città Nuova, Roma, 1971.
Giavini, G., "Relazione dello studio di gruppo sul libro: P. Grelot, Le ministere de la nouvelle alliance", *Riv. Bibl.,* 18, 1970.
Giblet, J., *Les Douze, Histoire et Theologie,* Grembloux, Paris, 1970.
Gihoul, Luc-Henri, Steckx, Raymond, "Foi et magistere", *Revue Nouvelle,* 49, 1969.
Girard-Reydet, J., "Le Pretre a la recherche de sa verite", *Pretre et Apotre,* 51, 1969.
Granfield, Patrick, "The Priesthood Today", *American Ecclesiastical Review,* 161, 1969.
Greeley, Andrew, "The Clergy of the Future", *Religion in the Year 2000,* Sheed and Ward, New York, 1969.
———, "After the Synod", *America,* November 20, 1971.
———, *Priests in the United States,* Doubleday, New York, 1971.
Grogan, Geoffrey W., "Christ and His People: an Exegetical and Theological Study of Hebrews 2:5-18", *Vox Evangelica,* 6, 1969.
Guillet, Charles-Marie, "L'Autorite dans le Peuple de Dieu", *Pretres Diocesains,* 107, 1969.

Hasenhuttl, G., *Les charismes dans la vie de l'Eglise,* Ed. du Cerf, Paris, 1970.

Haughey, John C., Campion, Donald R., "Bishops' Conferences Past and Present", *America,* 121, 1969.

Healy, John, "Why Older Priests need the Synod", *America,* Vol. 125, No. 8, September 25, 1971.

Hebblethwaite, Peter, Harriott, John F. X., "Synodal Diary", *The Month,* December 1971.

Hebblethwaite, Peter, *Understanding the Synod,* Logos, Dublin, 1968.

———, "The Synod on priests", *The Month,* December 1971.

———, "Synod Chronicle", *The Tablet,* 1971.

Herrero-Velarde, R., Arrieta, J. I., Ugalde, L., "Sinodo '71", *Sic,* Venezuela, 1971.

Heston, Edward, *The Priest of the Fathers,* Bruce, Milwaukee, 1945.

Hoekendijk, Hans, "Possibilites de structures radicalement differentes", *IDOC International,* 6, 1969.

Holstein, H., S.J., *Hierarchie et peuple de Dieu d'apres Lumen Gentium,* (Theologie historique, 12) Ed. Beauchesne, Paris.

"Hope for the Synod", *Commonweal,* Vol. XCV, No. 1, October 10, 1971.

Horgan, John, *The Church among the People,* Pflaum Press, Dayton, 1969.

Houtart, Francois, "Conflicts of Authority in the Roman Catholic Church", *Social Compass,* 16, 1969.

Hughes, John J., "On Anglican Orders", *The Ampleforth Journal,* Vol. LXXIII, Part II, Summer 1968.

Human Life in Our Day, United States Conference of Catholic Bishops, Washington, D.C., 1967.

"Interview with Cardinal Alfred Bengsch on the Priesthood", *CRIS,* Rome, No. 1, September 1971.

"Interview with Father Arrupe", *America,* Vol. 125, No. 3, August 1971.

"Introduction and Report on the Doctrinal Debate", *Herder Correspondence,* Vol. 6, No. 12, December 1969.

Jean-Nesmy, Claude, "Crise dans l'Eglise; question de foi", *Livres et Lectures,* 247, 1969.

Kaufmann, L., "The Ministerial Priesthood at the Bishops' Synod 1971", *The Clergy Review,* Vol. LVI, No. 8, August 1971.

Kerkhofs, Jan, "Begin van cen nieuw kerk-bele ven. De derde Romeinse Synode", *Streven,* December 1971.

Kjeseth, Peter, L, "Baptism as Ordination", *Dialog,* 8, 1969.

Kloppenburg, Boaventura, "O Sinodo dos Bispos, de 1971" *Revist Eclesiastica Brasileira,* 1971.

Klostermann, F., "Entmythologisierung des Priesterberufes und des Priesterberufung", *Gheologisches Jahrbuch,* Leipzig, St. Benno-Verlag, 1969.

———, "Principes d'une reforme de structures dans l'Eglise", *Pour une nouvelle image de l'Eglise,* Duculot, Gembloux, 1970.

Kohil, Kl., "Dogmatische Aussagen uber das Wesen Priestertums in der Verlautbarung der Papste Pius X, Pius XI and Pius XII", Diss. Univ., Innsbruck, 1970.

Kortenaar, Henry, "Go, and Synod no more", *Commonweal,* November 1971.

———, "Commonweal", Vol. XCV, No. 9, November 26, 1971.

———, "Commonweal", Vol. XCV, No. 8, October 1, 1971.

Krodel, Gerhard, "Forms and Functions of Ministries in the New Testament", *Dialog,* 8, 1969.

Krol, John Card., "A Study of the Priesthood in the US", *Catholic Mind,* Vol. LXIX, No. 1257, October 1971.

Küng, Hans, *The Theologian and the Church,* Sheed and Ward, London, 1965.

———, *Die Kirche,* Herder, Freiburg, 1967.

———, *The Church,* Burns & Oates, London, 1968.

———, "Mitentscheidung der laien in der Kirchenleitung und bei Kirchlichen Wahlan", *TQ.,* 149, 1969.

———, *Unfehlbar?,* Benziger, Einsiedeln, 1970.

———, *Wozu Priester?* Benziger, Einsiedeln, 1971.

———, *Infallibility? An Inquiry,* Doubleday, New York, 1971.

———, *Why Priests?* Collins, London, 1972.

Langevin, Gilles, "Le Mystere de I'Eglise", *La Foi et le temps; essais de theologie sur le second consile du Vatican,* Bruges, Desclee de Brouwer, 1969.

Laurentin, Rene, "Malgrè tout l'Esperance . . .", *Informations Catholiques Internationales,* November 15, 1971.

———, *"Apres le Synode ou va l'Eglise?",* January 1, 1972.

———, *Reorientation de l'Eglise apres le troisieme Synode,* Edit. du Seuil, Paris, 1972.

Lawlor, Francis, "Laity and Clergy According to Küng", *Homiletic and Pastoral Review,* Vol. LXXIII, No. 7, July 1973.

L'Attivita della Santa Sede nel 1969, Tipografia Poliglotta Vaticana, Vatican City, 1970.

L'Attività della Santa Sede nel 1971, Tipografia Poliglotta Vaticana, Vatican City, 1972.

"La Seconda assemblea generale del Sinodo dei Vescovi", *Annali d'Italia,* October-November 1971.

Lefevre, Lue J., "Notes et reflexions au cours du Synode des Eveques", *La Pensee Catholique,* No. 135, 1971.

———, "Quosque Tandem . . . Apres le Synode d'octobre", *La Pensee Catholique,* No. 136, January-February 1972.

Le Guillou, Marie-Joseph, O.P., "Il vero significato del Sinodo", *L'Osservatore Romano,* November 21, 1971.

Leloir, L., "Valeurs permanentes du sacerdoce levitique", *Nouv. Rev. Theol.,* 92, 1970.

Leroy, M.V., "L'Eglise de Hans Küng", *Rev. Thom.,* 70, 1970.

———, "Chronique d'ecclesiologie", *Revue Thomiste,* 69, 1969.

Lescrauwaet, J., M.S.C., "Drie theologische benaderingen van het dienstpriestchap", *Ons Geest,* Leven, 47, 1970.

"Le Sacre-College et le Synode sont complementaries", *Informations Catholiques Internationales,* 336, 1969, p. 7.

Lettera dei Vescovi Tedeschi sull'Ufficio Sacerdotal, Queriniana, Brescia, 1969.

Levi, Virgilio, "In margine al Sinodo dei vescovi: quattro protagonisti parlano del prete", *L'Osservatore della domenica,* November 14, 1971

Litalien, Rolland, "Nous avons lu: Le pretre de demain", *Eglise de Montreal,* 81, 1969.

Livio, Jean-Bernard, "Au coeur de la crise, l'espoir", *Choisir,* December 1971.

Lopez, Trujillo Alfonso, "Balance del Sinodo de los Obispos", *Revista Javeriana,* January, February 1972.

Lopez-Doriga, E., S.J., "Del Profetismo individual al Apostolado colegiado", *Libro Anual 1970,* Facultad de Teologia Pontificia y Civil, 4, Lima.

Lohfink, Norbert, "Ecclesial Ministry is Diversified", *Publik,* 8, Frankfurt, February 20, 1970.

Lukaszyk, Romuald, "Pojecie Kosciola jako Ludu Bozego w eklezjologil Vaticanum II", *Rockzniki Teologiczno-Kanoniczne,* 16 (z. 2, 1969).

Maccarrone, M., "Lo sviluppo dell'idea dell'episcopato nel II secolo e la formazione del simbolo della cattedra episcopale", *Problemi di Storia della Chiesa,* Ed. Vita e Pensiero, Milan, 1970.

Maggioni, B., "Il Sacerdozio nel Nuovo Testamento", *Rivista di Liturgia,* 56, 1969.

Magnani, Paolo, "Il contributo dei vescovi italiani al recente Sinodo sul tema del sacerdozio ministeriale", *La Rivista del clero italiano,* 1972.

Manaranche, Andre, *Al servicio de los hombres,* Sigueme, Salamanca, 1969.
Mangiavacchi, Sergio, "Un parroco al Sinodo", *Orientamenti pastorali,* 1971.
Marranzini, A., "Problematica teologica del sacerdozio", *Rass. di Teol.,* 11, 1970.
———, "Note informative e bibliografiche sul sacerdozio ministeriale", *Presenza pastorale,* 1971.
Marsh, Thomas, "The Social Role of a Bishop", *Furrows,* Vol. 22, No. 8, August 1971.
Marty, Francis Card., "Le Pretre devra toujours etre serviteur de l'Evangile", *L'Osservatore Romano,* 1031, 1969.
Mascall, E. L., *The Secularization of Christianity,* Holt, Rienhart and Winston, New York, 1966.
Mateo-Seco, L. F., "Sacerdocio de los fieles y sacerdocio ministerial en san Gregorio de Nisa", *Teologia del Sacerdocio. Sacerdocio ministerial y laical,* Ed. Aldecoa, Burgos, 1970.
Mauer, Otto, "3 Wochen Bischofssynode", *Actio Catholica,* Vienna, 1971.
Medeiros, Humberto, Card., "The Ministerial Priesthood" (Pastoral Letter), Daughters of St. Paul, Boston, 1971.
Mejia, Jorge, "El tercer Sinode de los Obispos", *Criterio,* 1971.
———, "Anticipaciones sobre el Sinode, *Criterio,* 1971.
———, "El Sinodo: conclusion y panorama general", *Criterio,* 1971.
———, "Los probelmas del sacerdocio en el Sinodo", *Criterio,* 1971.
"Members of the Second General Assembly of the Synod of Bishops", *L'Osservatore Romano* (English), September 30, 1971.
Migne, Jacques-Paul (ed.), *Patrologiae cursus completus, series latina,* 221 vols., Paris, 1844-1864.
———, *Patrologiae cursus completus, series graeca,* 161 vols., Paris 1857-1866.
Milano, A., "Il Sacerdozio nella Ecclesiologia de St. Tommaso d'Aquino", *Asprenas,* 17, 1970.
Mission and Witness, (ed.), Patrick Burnes, Chapman, London, 1965.
Mohler, J. A., S.J., *The origin and evolution of the priesthood: a return to the sources,* Alba House, Staten Island, 1969.
Moingt, J., "Priestly Character and Ministry", *Theology* Digest, 17, 1969.
———, "Nature du sacerdoce ministeriel", *Rech. Sc. Rel.,* 58, 1970.
Montorsi, G., *Il sacerdote dopo il concillo Vaticano II,* Dehoniane, Bologna, 1969.
Moreno, Judas, "Lecciones del Sinodo pasado. El P. Liege habla para H. D.", *Hechos y Dichos,* January 1972.

Morissette, Gaston, "Primitive Eglise, edition 1969", *Revue Eucharistique du Clerge,* 72, 1969.

Morsdorf, Klaus, "Jurisdiction", *Sacramentum Mundi: an encyclopedia of theology,* Palm Publ., Montreal, 1969.

———, "Hierarchy", *Sacramentum Mundi: an encyclopedia of theology,* Palm Publ., Montreal, 1969.

Muhlsteiger, J., S.J., "Sanctorum Communio", *Zeitsch. Kath. Theol.,* 92, 1970.

Murphy, Francis X., *Synod 67 a New Sound in Rome,* Bruce, Milwaukee, 1968.

———, "The Priest in Search of his Humanity", *Tablet,* May 15, 1971.

———, "The Priestly Ministry and the Roman Synod 1971", *IDOC,* April 27, 1971.

———, "The Roman Synod of Bishops 1971", *American Ecclesiastical Review,* Vol. CLXV, No. 2, October 1971.

McBrien, Richard, *Do We Need the Church?* Collins, London, 1969.

McCarthy, John, "Ecclesiology in the Letters of St. Ignatius of Antioch: A Textual Analysis", *American Benedictine Review,* Vol. XXIII, No. 3, September 1971.

McGrath, Marco Gregorio, "Rapport sur les relations des conferences episcopales entre elles", *L'Osservatore Romano* 1037, 12, 1969.

McKenzie, John L., *L'Autorità nella Chiesa; esame critico e nuove prospettive,* Cribaudi, Torino, 1969.

McKeon, Richard M., "Service, Yes—Dissipation, No!, *Pastoral Life* 17, 1969.

McNamara, Kevin, "The Theological Position of a Bishop", *Furrows,* Vol. 22, No. 8, August 1971.

Naveillan, C., "El 3er Sinodo Romano", *Mensaje,* 1971.

Nelson, J. R., "Toward an Ecumenical Ecclesiology", *Theol. Studies,* t. 31, 1970.

Newman, Manning, "Priesthood in Crisis", *Priest,* 25, 1969.

Nicolau, M., *O Sacerdote conforme o Vaticano II,* Ed. Paulans, Sao Paolo, 1969.

Nijk, A. J., "Horizontal—vertikaal: reeél dilemma of dubieus denkschema", *Rondom het Woord,* 11, 1969.

O'Brien, John A., "Service", *Pastoral Life,* 17, 1969.

Ochoa, Xaverius, *Index Verborum cum documentis Concilii Vaticani Secundi,* Rome, 1967.

O'Donnell, Desmond, "New Directions in Priestly and Religious Living", *Review for Religious,* 28, 1969.

O'Grady, Colm, "Hans Küng's Ecumenical Programme: An Enquiry", *The Clergy Review,* Vol. LVI, No. 12, December 1971.

O'Reilly, Thomas A., "Priest of the 70's", *Homiletic and Pastoral Review,* 69, 1968-69.

Orsy, Ladislas, "The Priest Center of Unity in the Christian Community", *America,* Vol. 125, No. 8, September 25, 1971.

Paphnuce, "Perspectives post-synodales", *La Revue Nouvelle,* 1972.

"Per la Chiesa la Missione non è un Lusso", *La Civiltà Cattolica,* Ann. 122, Vol. 4, 1971.

Picard, P., "Sur le sacrament de l'ordre", *Bulletin du Comite des Etudes,* 1969.

Piero, B., "Ortodossia dottrinale o gruppo di potere nella Chiesa", *Mulino,* 18, 1969.

Pignatiello, L., "La peculiarità essenziale del sacerdozio ministeriale. Implicazioni ascetiche e pastorali", *Asprenas,* 17, 1970.

Pironio, E., "Reflexion teologica sobre el sacerdote", *Teologia* (Buenos Aires), 8, n. 7.

Polley, George Warren, "Ordination: Enslavement or Freedom?", *Foundations,* 12, 1969.

Predazzi, Giuseppe, "Bilancio di un Sinodo di transizione", *Idea,* January 1972.

"Preti Nuovi per un Mondo Nuovo", *La Civiltà Cattolica,* Ann. 122, Vol. 4, 1971.

"Priest Auditors of the Synod of Bishops", *Catholic Mind,* Vol LXIX, No. 1225.

Puccinelli, Mario, Stracca, Silvano, "Il Sinodo dei vescovi", *La Rivista del clero italiano,* 1972.

Quadri, "Riflessioni sul sacerdozio ministeriale nel momento attuale", *Riv. Clero Italiano,* 51, 1970.

Quesnell, Quentin, "St. Paul on Earning a Living", *Hyphenated Priests,* (ed.) W. H. Cleavy, Corpus Publ., Washington, 1969.

Radermakers, Jean, "La Mission Engagement Radical", *Nouvelle Revue Theologique,* No. 10, November 1971.

Rahazzotti, B., "Il Ministero Ecclesiastico nella Luce della Bibbia e del Vaticano II", *Doctor Communis,* 23, 1970.

Rahner, Karl, "L'Eveque et le diocese", *Mystere de L'Eglise et action* pastorale, Desclee, Paris, 1969.

———, "Magisterium", *Sacramentum Mundi: an encyclopedia of theology,* Palm Publ., Montreal, 1969.

———, *Theological Investigations: Volume 6 Concerning Vatican Council II,* Helicon Press, Baltimore, 1969.

———, "Schism in the Church?", *Month,* 228, 1969.

———, "La Grace du sacerdoce", *Serviteurs du Christ,* Mame, Tours, 1969.

Rahner, Karl and Vorgrimler, Herbert, *Theological Dictionary,* Herder, New York, 1965.

"Rahner-Küng Debate", *Homiletic and Pastoral Review,* Vol. LXXI, Nos. 8, 9, 10 and 11, 1970.
Rambaldi, G., S.I., "Natura e missione del Presbiterato nel decreto 'Presbyterorum Ordinis' N. 2: Genesi e contenuto del testo", *Greg.,* 50, 1969.
Rapport de la Commission Internationale de Theologie, "Le Ministere sacerdotal", Cerf, Paris, 1971.
Ratzinger, J., *Das nueu Volk Gottes; Entzurfe zur Ekklesiologie.* Patmos, Dusseldorf, 1969.
Relazioni e Documenti della VI Assemblea Generale Della C.E.I., "Il Sacerdozio Ministeriale", Studium, Rome, 1971.
"Recontre de la Congregation pour la Doctrine de la Foi avec des representants de Commissions doctrinales des Conferences episcopales", *L'Osservatore Romano,* 1039, 1969.
Report of the National Opinion Research Center, "American Priests", Chicago, March 1971.
"Responsabilite sacerdotale dans le monde moderne", *Masses Ouvrieres,* 263, 1969.
Ribeiro, I., Montiero, J., "O Ill Sinodo", *Broteria,* 1971.
Ricci, Giovanni, "Il Sinodo nella stampa quotidiana italiana", *Orientamenti sociali,* 1971.
Richard, Richard, *Secularization Theology, Herder,* New York, 1967.
Riquet, Michel, "Crise de l'Eglise et Synode", *La Nouvelle Revue des deux Mondes,* November 1971.
Rodrigues, Manuel, "The Future Priest", *Seminaire,* 34, 1969.
Rolla, A., "Il sacerdozio ministeriale nella Ribbia. Continuità e rottura con l'ambiente", *Asprenas,* 17, 1970.
Romani, Joseph, "Priest of the 70's", *Homiletic and Pastoral Review,* 69, 1968-69.
Romaniuk, C., "Il sacerdozio nel Nuovo Testamento. Esegesi e tradizione", *La Spiritualità Sacerdotale,* N. 9, Edizioni Dehoniane, Bologna, 1970.
Romita, Florentino (ed.), *Concilii Oecumenici Vaticani II,* Constitutiones Decreta-Declarationes, Rome, 1967.
Routh, Porter, "Ordination: contemporary problems", *Southwestern Journal of Theology,* 11, Spring 1969.
———, "La vexata quaestio del celibato ecclesiastico al Sinodo di ottobre", *Idea,* February 1972.
Rubin, Ladislao, "A Realizacao dos Votos de Sinodo Episcopal", *Revista Ecleslastica Brasileira,* 29, 1969.
Rubio, Luis, Cabezas, Julio, "Presbiterio y communidades sacerdotales", Seminarios, 15, 1969.

Russo, B., "Natura e origine del potere dei vescovi", *Rassegna di Teologia,* II, 1970.
Rynne, Xavier, *The Second Session,* Straus, New York, 1964.
The Sacred Ministry, (ed.) G. R. Runstan, S.P.C.K., 1970.
Salaun, R., "Que s'est-t-il done passe au Synode", *Lettre aux Communautes de la Mission de Françe, 1972,* n. 31, pp. 23-49; *Vocation,* 1972, n. 257, pp. 123-135.
Sanchez De Rojas, M., "Las Crisis y defecciones sacerdotales: sus remedios", *Palabra,* 46, 1969.
Sanchez Y Sanchez, J., "Centralizacion y descentralizacion (Curia Romana y Conferencias episcopales)", *Dinamica juridica postconciliar,* Consejo Superior de Investigaciones Cientificas, Salamanca, 1969.
Sanchis, Ricardo, "El Sinodo de Obispos, encrucijada de la Iglesia", *Hechos y Dichos,* November 1971.
———, "El Sinodo de Obispos. Balance: desencanto y esperanza", *Hechos y Dichos,* December 1971.
Santidrian, Tomas A., "Algunos aspectos del sacerdocio en el Sinodo", *Criterio* (Buenos Aires), 1972.
Savard, Aime: "Le Synode: une photographie de l'Eglise en 1971", *Informations Catholiques Internationales,* December 1, 1971.
———, "Des 'conciles nationaux': pourquoi pas?", *Informations Catholiques Internationales,* 330, 1969.
Scandone, Alberto, "La Chiesa cattolica all'ora del Sinodo", *Rinascita,* September 17, 1971.
———, "La volontà restauratrice del Sinodo", *Rinascita,* November 12, 1971.
Schelkle, Karl Hermann, "Ministry and Minister in the New Testament Church", *Concilium* (English), 5, March 1969.
———, "New Testament Theology. II. Pauline Theology. E. The Church", *Sacramentum Mondi: an encyclopedia of theology,* Palm Publ., Montreal, 1969.
Schmaus, M., "Il sacerdozio: sua natura, suo compito", *Renovatio,* 5, 1970.
Schillebeeckx, Edward, "Synode, gouvernement collegial et Eglise locale", *IDOC International,* 8, 1969.
———, "Theologie des kirchlichen Amtes", *Diakonia-Seelsorger,* I, 1970.
Schmitt, E., Kein "Konzil im Kleinformat", *Materialdienst des Konfessionskunlichen Instituts Bensdeim,* Nov.-Dec. 1971.
Schmitt, Paul-Joseph, "Document on Priestly Ministry", *Documentation Catholique,* January 16, 1972.
Schmitz, van Vorst, Josef, "Il Sinodo è andato controcorrente?", *L'Osservatore Romano,* 21, November 1971.

Schnackenburg, Rudolf, *The Church in the New Testament,* Burns and Oates, London, 1965.

Schuller, D. S., *Power Structures and the Church,* Concordia, London, 1969.

Seltz, Anne-Marie, "Le pretre a l'heure du Synode mondial", *Criterio* (Buenos Aires), 1972.

Setien, Jose Maria, "Tensions in the Church", *Concilium* (American) 48, 1969.

Sharper, Philip, "As Others See Us: the Priest in Trouble", *Priest,* 25, 1969.

Sheerin, John, "The Synod—Hope Deferred", *Catholic World,* Vol. 214, No. 1281.

Shehan, Lawrence, Card., "Priests in the Church of Today", *Priest,* 25, 1969.

Siefkes, J. A., "Holy Politics", *Lutheran Quarterly,* 21, 1969.

Simon, Louis, "Contribution biblique a une critique du clerge", *Freres du Monde,* 61-62, 1969.

Simonet, Andre, *The Priest and His Bishop,* Herder, St. Louis, 1969.

Smith, J., *A Priest for Ever; a study of typology and eschatology in Hebrews,* Sheed and Ward, London, 1969.

Stam, J., "Episcopacy in the Apostolic Tradition of Hippolytus", *Theol. Diss.,* Reinhardt, Basel, 1969.

"Statement, House of Delegates, N.F.P.C.", *Catholic Mind,* Vol. LXIX, No. 1254.

Studer, B., "Ill sacerdozio dei fedeli in sant' Ambrogio di Milano", *Vetera Christianorum,* 7, 1970.

Swain, Lionel, "The Debate on Priesthood", *Clergy Review,* 1969.

"Synod of Bishops Stearing Wheel or Brake", *Clergy Review,* Vol. LVI, No. 9, September 1971.

Tange, A., *Analyse psychologique de l'Eglise,* Ed. Fleurus, Paris, 1970.

Tettamanzi, D., "Saggio bibliografico sul ministero e la vita sacerdotale", *Asprenas,* 17, 1970.

"Theses sur l'Ordination (1969)", *Christianisme Social,* 718, 1969.

Thils, Gustave, "Le Magistere du College episcopal", *L'Infallibilite pontificale, source, conditiones, limites,* Duculot, Gembloux, 1969.

Thomas, Joseph, "Le Synode, moment de verite", *Christus,* January 1972.

———, "Pouvoirs du Synode", *Recherches et debats,* June 1972.

Thurian, M., *Sacerdoce et ministere,* Presses de Taize, Taize, 1970.

———, *Il sacerdozio ministeriale,* d'Auria, Napoli, 1970.

Triggs, William, "The Synod of Bishops: new era or disillusion?", *The Christian Century,* 1971.

Urs von Balthasar Hans, "Zur Priesterfrage an der Bischofssynode 1971", Internationale Katholische Zeitschrift, 1972.

———, "Bischofssynode 1971", *Das Priesteramt, Sammlung Kriterien,* Johannes Verlag, Einsiedeln, 1972.

Van Beeck, Frans Josef, "Sacraments, Church Order, and Secular Responsibility", *Theological Studies,* 30, 1969.

Vekemans, Roger, *Caesar and God,* Orbis, New York, 1972.

Villinger, Johann, Baptist, "Bilanz der dritten Bischofssynode", *Schweizerische Krichen Zeitune,* 1971.

van Galli, Marius, "Brief aus Rom. Die Bischofssynode in Rom", *Orientierune,* 1971.

Walter, Julian, "Priest or Minister", *Month,* Vol. CCXXXII, No. 1250, October 1971.

Wasselynck, Rene, "Journal clinique du pretre francais 1962-1969", *Vocation,* 247, 1969.

Watte, Pierre, "Diagnostics sur la crise de l'Eglise", *Revue Nouvelle* 50, 1969.

Weber, Johann, "Rückblick auf die dritte Bischofssynode in Rom", *Schweizerische Kirchen Zeitung,* 1972.

Woodrow, Alai, "Le Synode vu de Rome", *Informations Catholiques Internationale,* October 15, 1971, pp. 3-6, November 1, 1971, pp. 13-16, November 15, 1971, pp. 6-9.

———, "Bilan du Synode", December 1, 1971, pp. 6-9.

———, "Le Texte sur le pretres formule des regles, plus qu'il n'incite a l'action apostolique", *Informations Catholiques Internationales,* December 1, 1971.

Wright, John Card., "Il Sacerdote e la Societa, Secolarizzata", *Secolarizazione et Sacerdozio,* Ares, Milano, 1969.

———, "Sacerdozio e Umanesimo", *Sacerdozio et Senso della Vita,* Ares, Milan, 1970.

———, "Priestly Maturity", *Seminarium,* Anno X, N. 3, July 1970.

———, "Christ Head of the Church and the Priest", *Seminarium,* Anno X, N. 1, January 1970.

———, *Coscienza e Autorità,* Città Nuova, Rome, 1970.

———, "Cultura e Formazione del Clero", *Studi Pastorali,* Vol. XIV, February 1970.

———, "La Formazione Sociale del Clero", *Monitor Ecclesiasticus,* Vol. IV, April 1970.

———, "La Persona Umana Davanti agli Umanesimi di Oggi", *Studi Cattolici,* December 1971.

———, *The Church Hope of the World,* Prow, Kenosha, 1972.

Wuerl, Donald, "Natural Law, the Community and Authority", *Priest,* Vol. 25, No. 5, May 1969.

———, "Synods Past and Future", *Priest,* Vol. 26, No. 4, April 1970.
———, "Priest's Councils", *L'Osservatore Romano* (English), No. 30, 121, July 23, 1970.
———, "Witness and the Church", *American Ecclesiastical Review,* Vol. 163, No. 3, September 1970.
———, "Priest as Politician in the United States", *L'Osservatore Romano,* N. 47 (138) November 1970, English Edition.
———, "Priest, Prophet and the Political Party", *American Ecclesiastical Review,* Vol. 166, No. 8, October 1972.
———, "The third synod of bishops on the ministerial priesthood", *Homiletic and Pastoral Review,* January 1972.
———, "Problem of the Priest-Politician", *Homiletic and Pastoral Review,* Vol. LXXII, No. 6, March 1973.
———, "Paix et Developpement social", *Nouveaux Rythmes du Monde,* Vol. 1, No. 1, 1973.
———, "Pastoral Councils", *Homiletic and Pastoral Review,* Vol. LXXIII, Nos. 11-12, August-September 1973.
Yarnold, E.J., "Küng Examined", *Month,* Vol. CCXXXII, 1249, September 1971.
Zedda, S., "Sacerdozio e ministri nel Nuovo Testamento", *Asprenas,* 17, 1970.
Zoungrana, Paul Card., "Conference de presse sur le resserrement des liens entre Conferences episcopales elles-memes", *L'Osservatore* Romano, 1038, 1969.
———, "Intervention (au Synode sur les Conferences episcopales)", *L'Osservatore Romano,* 1037, 1969.